THE CANTERBURY QUADRANGLE

The east frontispiece of the Canterbury Quadrangle (*Thomas Photos*)

The
Canterbury Quadrangle

St John's College
Oxford

HOWARD COLVIN

OXFORD UNIVERSITY PRESS
1988

Oxford University Press, Walton Street, Oxford OX2 6DP
Oxford New York Toronto
Delhi Bombay Calcutta Madras Karachi
Petaling Jaya Singapore Hong Kong Tokyo
Nairobi Dar es Salaam Cape Town
Melbourne Auckland
and associated companies in
Berlin Ibadan

Oxford is a trade mark of Oxford University Press

Published in the United States
by Oxford University Press, New York

British Library Cataloguing in Publication Data
Colvin, H. M.
The Canterbury Quadrangle.
1. St John's College (University of
Oxford)—Canterbury Quadrangle
2. Oxford (Oxfordshire)—Buildings,
structures, etc.
I. Title
727'.3'0942574   LF696
ISBN 0–19–920159–5

Library of Congress Cataloging in Publication Data
Colvin, Howard Montagu.
The Canterbury Quadrangle.
Includes index.
1. St. John's College (University of Oxford)—
Description.   I. Title.
LF696.C65   1988   378.425'74   87–23954
ISBN 0–19–920159–5

Set by Promenade Graphics Ltd., Cheltenham
Printed in Great Britain
at the University Printing House, Oxford
by David Stanford
Printer to the University

PREFACE

THIS book has developed out of a lecture given in June 1986 to commemorate the 350th anniversary of the completion of the Canterbury Quadrangle. Besides setting out more fully the evidence upon which that lecture was based, I have added sections on the Library, the President's Lodgings, the rooms in the quadrangle, and changing attitudes towards the problems presented by the maintenance of a historic building still in active use.

I am grateful to the Governing Body for giving me the opportunity to explore the architectural history of one of Oxford's most celebrated quadrangles, and to Mr K. V. Thomas, now President of Corpus Christi College, for his help and encouragement. I have benefited in various ways from the expertise of my colleagues Dr Kenneth Fincham, Dr Peter Hacker, Mr S. J. Harrison, Mr Nicholas Purcell, and Professor D. A. F. M. Russell. Dr Rosalys Coope has provided valuable information about French architectural sources, Mr David Sturdy about seventeenth-century craftsmen, and Mr Adam White about sculptors. Others to whom I am indebted for help in various ways are Dr Ian Campbell of the Bibliotheca Herziana in Rome, Mr Michael Dudley of the Ashmolean Museum's photographic studio, Dr G. M. King of the University Museum, Mr F. R. Maddison of the Museum of the History of Science, Mr John Newman of the Courtauld Institute of Art, Mr Peter Smith of the Royal Commission on the Ancient and Historical Monuments of Wales, Mr Anthony Wells-Cole of the Temple Newsam Museum, Leeds, and Miss Angela Williams of St John's College Library.

H.M.C.

St John's College, Oxford
December 1986

CONTENTS

LIST OF ILLUSTRATIONS

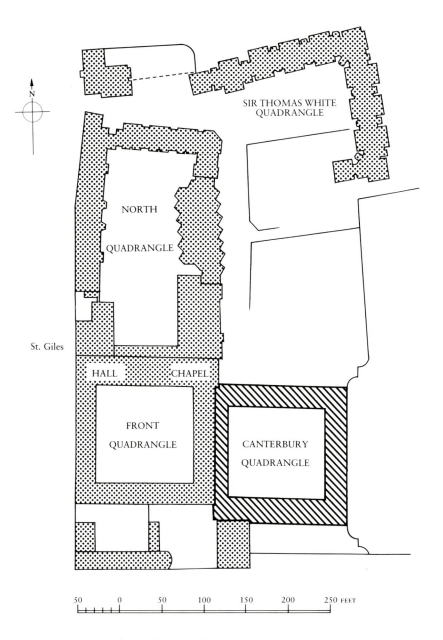

N

SIR THOMAS WHITE
QUADRANGLE

NORTH

QUADRANGLE

St. Giles

HALL   CHAPEL

FRONT

QUADRANGLE

CANTERBURY

QUADRANGLE

50   0   50   100   150   200   250 FEET

1. Block plan of St John's College, showing the position of the
Canterbury Quadrangle

1.

The Building of the Canterbury Quadrangle

IT is difficult to envisage St John's College without the Canterbury Quadrangle. For 350 years the Canterbury Quadrangle has been as essential a part of the College's architectural identity as its hall is to Christ Church, its chapel to New College, or its tower to Magdalen. In a university built round quadrangles it stands out as one of the most ambitious of its kind, and as the first in which the architecture is predominantly classical.

But for the first forty years after its foundation in 1555, St John's consisted only of the single quadrangle built in the fifteenth century for the Cistercian monks of St Bernard's College, and acquired by its Founder, Sir Thomas White, after the monks had been dispossessed by King Henry VIII. In that quadrangle there were only about twenty rooms, but the Founder intended the College to have fifty fellows in all. It was some time before that total was reached, and in the 1570s the accommodation was increased by forming rooms in the roofs; but any vacant space was taken up by commoners, and once there were fifty fellows in residence, as was the case from 1583 onwards, it would have been necessary for all but the most favoured to share with one or two others. As the College was far from well off, most of the fellows of St John's in the late sixteenth century lived cramped and penurious lives. The library, moreover, was small, and there must have been considerable competition for the limited stock of books, which were kept in a room on the east side of the quadrangle.

A larger library was one of the College's first priorities. In 1573 there was talk of getting the Surveyor of the Queen's Works to come down and advise the College about building a new library,[1] but in fact it was not until 1596 that this became possible. With the aid of the Merchant Taylors' Company and of other benefactors a large new library was erected on a site to the east of the old quadrangle. It occupied the upper floor of a Tudor Gothic building whose ground floor provided four new sets of rooms. For some reason that is not now clear, it did not immediately adjoin the old quadrangle, but it was so sited that it could be incorporated in the south side of a future second quadrangle.[2] It was linked to the

---

[1] W. H. Stevenson and H. E. Salter, *Early History of St John's College* (1939), 198. The Surveyor at the time was Lewis Stockett. [2] See below, pp. 56–7.

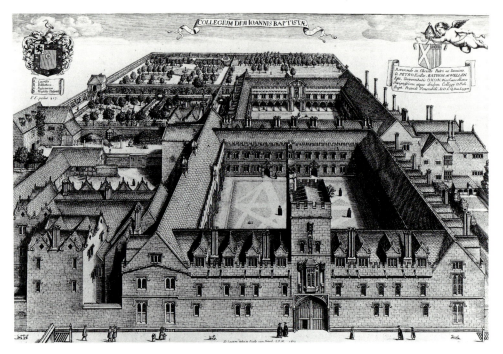

2. View of St John's College from the west, from Loggan's *Oxonia Illustrata* (1675)

old quadrangle by some sort of cloister, over or adjoining which further rooms were built in 1599–1601.[3] The west side of these rooms can be seen on the right in Loggan's engraved view of 1675 (Fig. 2).

As President of St John's from 1611 to 1621, William Laud would have been well aware of the constraints of academic life at the College and of the need for more accommodation. His affection for St John's was genuine. He prided himself on having 'governed that College in peace, without so much as the show of a faction, all my time'.[4] When he became Bishop of St David's it was to the patron saint of his old College that he dedicated the chapel he had built at his episcopal residence at Abergwili.[5] In 1642, a prisoner in the Tower, he had a nightmare about Oxford being in Parliamentary hands and St John's in ruins;[6] and when he was executed his last wish was to be buried in the College Chapel.[7]

So it was natural that when, in 1630, Laud, by now Bishop of London and Chancellor of the University, considered how best to devote some of his wordly wealth to charity, he should have thought of paying for a new building at St John's. But more than *pietas* was involved in the decision.

[3] College Archives, *Computus Annuus* 1598–1604, fos. 27, 83.

[4] Laud, *Works*, ed. P. Bliss (1847–60) vi, 89.

[5] 'I named it the Chapel of St. John Baptist, in grateful remembrance of St. John Baptist College in Oxford, of which I had been first Fellow, and afterwards President' (ibid. iii, 171).

[6] Ibid. iii, 246.

[7] Ibid. iv, 442.

By this time Laud was a dominant figure in both Church and State. The old Archbishop of Canterbury, George Abbott, was more or less in disgrace, and Laud had the King's entire confidence both as a churchman and as a statesman. His attempt to impose on an unruly and divided country his vision of an ordered society united in obedience and loyalty to an autocratic monarchy is beyond the scope of this book, but his role as a great political prelate is relevant to the Canterbury Quadrangle, for it was to be a permanent memorial of his high standing in Church and State.

There was another reason why Laud's charitable impulses should have been directed towards his old College. Fundamental to his policies as a churchman was a determination to win back for the Church as much as possible of what it had lost as a result of the Reformation—in endowments, in dignity, and in authority. It was therefore natural that in bestowing his own charity he should look to pre-Reformation precedents rather than to those of the more recent past. In recent years episcopal charity had tended to conform to current fashion in founding grammar schools and almshouses, of which Archbishop Whitgift's School at Croydon and Archbishop Abbott's Hospital at Guildford were notable examples.

But what the great pre-Reformation prelates had done was to build colleges at Oxford—Wykeham at New College, Chichele at All Souls, Waynflete at Magdalen, Wolsey at Christ Church. For more reasons than one Laud was not quite in the same league financially as a Wykeham or a Wolsey (for one thing he was a much more scrupulous man than either of them), so to found a new college might well have been beyond his resources. But to add a second quadrangle to St John's was within his capacity as well as something close to his heart as a former President of the College. It would, moreover, proclaim to the world that the clothier's son from Reading had risen to be Chancellor of the University and one of the greatest men in the land after the King himself.

The scheme that formed itself in Laud's mind in 1630 was architecturally fairly simple (Fig. 3). It was to erect 'a range of buildings opposite to the Library', and to build 'a high wall to joyne them at the east end', with 'a cloister upon pillars under the dead wall'.[8] The mention of pillars implies that the cloister was to be classical in style, but Laud's memorandum indicates that there was to be a Gothic bay-window at the east end to match the one at the end of the library, and that both the existing library wing and the new one were to be battlemented.[9]

---

[8] PRO, SP16/172, fo. 68: endorsed 'My intentions for Charity soe soone as God shall make me able'.

[9] The Front Quadrangle had been battlemented in 1617 at the expense of Thomas and Benjamin Henshaw, whose arms commemorate their generosity, but the north side of the library was so far without battlements, as the south side still is.

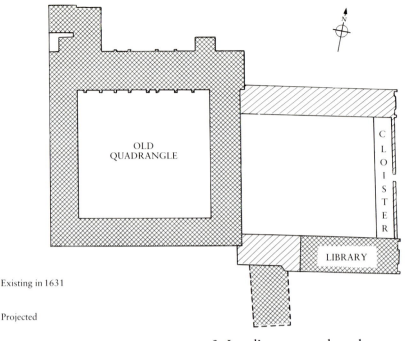

OLD
QUADRANGLE

C
L
O
I
S
T
E
R

LIBRARY

N

Existing in 1631

Projected

3. Laud's new quadrangle, as envisaged in 1630

4. Miniature drawing of a monastery, with features resembling Laud's original scheme for the Canterbury Quadrangle: from a manuscript of *c.*1630 (Magdalene College, Cambridge, Pepysian Library MS 2258, by permission of the Master and Fellows)

Although quadrangles had long been the rule at Oxford, parallel ranges joined only by a screen wall were not uncommon in English country-house architecture, and one Cambridge college, Caius, had been built on this plan, though without a cloister. As it happens a contemporary drawing showing just such an arrangement can be seen in a manuscript in the Pepysian Library at Cambridge (Fig. 4). And when we discover that this manuscript was a copy, with new illustrations, of a fifteenth-century manuscript (now in the Bodleian) that actually belonged to Laud in the 1630s, it is tempting to suggest that what we are looking at is an artist's impression of the original scheme for the Canterbury Quadrangle, though what it actually purports to show is a medieval monastery.[10]

[10] For the relationship between Pepys MS 2258 and MS Laud misc. 740 see R. Tuve, *Allegorical Imagery* (Princeton, 1966), 214–15, where the possible relevance of the drawing to the Canterbury Quadrangle is pointed out.

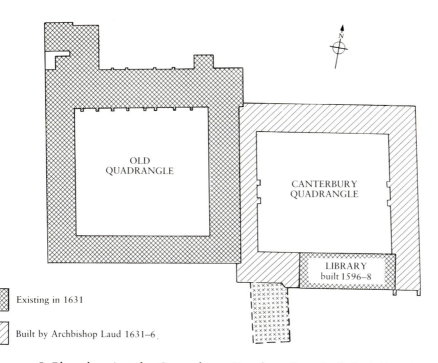

OLD
QUADRANGLE

CANTERBURY
QUADRANGLE

LIBRARY
built 1596–8

Existing in 1631

Built by Archbishop Laud 1631–6

5. Plan showing the Canterbury Quadrangle as built in 1631–6

It was presumably on this basis that work began in the summer of 1631. On 15 April the College gratefully accepted Laud's proposal to 'beautify the east part of the College with a new building', giving him leave 'to proceede in the worke as soon as hee shall please, according to the platt forme projected, or, if neede be, to alter the same in anie point which may make for the better convenience or uniformitie of the building'.[11] An estimate indicated a total expenditure of £1,005, a gift of timber from the royal woods at Shotover was solicited and granted, and a contract was made with an Oxford mason called Richard Maude.[12] The foundation-stone was laid on 26 July and some £700 was spent in the course of the following months.[13]

The mason's contract was evidently for the north range only, and early in 1632 William Juxon, as President of the College, was in correspondence with Laud about the next stage. With Laud's encouragement, a more ambitious scheme was now envisaged (Fig. 5). Instead of just two parallel ranges joined by a screen wall, there was now to be a complete new quadrangle with arcaded cloisters on both east and west sides. In

[11] College Register, iii, fo. 69. See also the fulsome letter of thanks addressed to Laud (in Latin) on the same day (PRO, SP 16/188, no. 66).
[12] For the estimate see PRO, SP 16/186, fo. 110, and for the timber ibid. fo. 12, and the Building Accounts (College Archives, lxxxi. 2), pp. 72–6. The royal gift amounted in the end to 293 tons.

[13] For the foundation-stone see Laud's Diary (*Works*, iii, 214) and Building Accounts, p. 80. For the expenditure see President Juxon's receipts for money received from Laud in PRO, SP 16/191–211, itemized in *Cal. S. P. Dom. 1631–3*, pp. 21, 135, 181, 276.

order to accommodate the new west range and keep the quadrangle roughly square, it was decided to move the east side out, adding some twenty feet both to the north range and to the old library. The cloisters, Juxon wrote, would be 'of the largest size that Art can allowe', and 'of a forme not yet seene in Oxford'. Over the east range there was to be an extension of the library, over the western a gallery attached to the President's Lodgings. All this, Juxon reported, could be done for £3,200. 'For the summe aforesaid', he assured Laud, 'your Lordshipp shall have a perfect new Quadrangle.'[14]

A new masonry contract was now necessary. Unfortunately its text has not survived, but we know that it included 'the two cloister sides and fronts'—that is, the two central features that were to be the architectural climax of the quadrangle—and that, faced with a much more considerable task, Maude now took two partners, Robert Smith and Hugh Davies.[15] The new design was embodied in a model, made by the Oxford joiner David Woodfield and delivered to the President's Lodgings on 1 June.[16] Meanwhile the carpenter's contract for the north range had been signed in April.[17] But all did not go well with the masons: their work lagged behind, and in August 1633 they abandoned their contract, leaving the north range still incomplete and elements of the cloisters in various states of preparation. Another mason called William Hill took over and undertook to complete Maude and Co.'s contract for £686, but proved equally unsatisfactory and had to be discharged early in 1634 after doing work valued at only £394.[18]

The reason for these failures is not clear. When Laud asked for an investigation Maude and his partners soon admitted that their difficulties were due to 'their own improvidence and indiscretion', begged for lenient treatment, and were in fact given an *ex gratia* payment of £170 to save them from financial disaster.[19] One suspects that the need to cut unfamiliar classical mouldings and other such features may have been a contributory factor. The accounts more than once refer to the remaking of pillars which had been cut to the wrong size by Hill or his predecessors.[20] But in the seventeenth century building by contract was generally

[14] PRO, SP 16/214, fos 38 and 49 (printed below, pp. 115–16).

[15] Building Accounts, p. 6, 'their last Bargaine for the 2 Cloister sides & Fronts, with all the odde workes in the ould Quadrangle, & in the President's Lodginge'; PRO, SP 16/250, fo. 45, report of Heads of Colleges to Laud, referring to 'two severall bargaines drawne into distinct articles', the first with Maude alone for the north side, the second with Maude, Davies, and Smith for the south, west, and east sides.

[16] Building Accounts, pp. 65, 81. For Woodfield, see below, p. 82 n.

[17] Building Accounts, p. 36.

[18] Ibid. 5–7, 82, 84, etc. Hill was evidently not an Oxford man: see p. 82, 11 Sept. 1633.

[19] PRO, SP 16/248, fo. 80, 250, fo. 45, 251, fo. 40. See also the record of the action brought against the masons by their sureties in the Chancellor's Court (Oxford University Archives 1633/81: 1–3 and p. 53b).

[20] Building Accounts, p. 23.

6. The west side of the Canterbury Quadrangle

regarded as a risky proceeding; for contractors could easily miscalculate, and then (as Sir Christopher Wren put it) 'they shuffle and slight the work to save themselves'.[21] It was, as the fellows of St John's College, Cambridge, had found a few years earlier, 'a way of building not so allowable in works intended for posterity'.[22] By 1634 their counterparts at Oxford had learnt the same lesson, and the work on the Canterbury Quadrangle was put on a new footing. Henceforward it was to be carried on partly by direct labour, partly by measure, and partly by piece-work, all under the direction of an experienced master mason. This necessitated the keeping of detailed accounts by the fellow of the College, John Lufton, to whom Laud had entrusted the supervision of his building, so from 1634 onwards we are much more fully informed about the progress of the works than we are for the previous three years.

Lufton's responsibilities were now greatly increased. He was not only paymaster and accountant, but recruiter of labour, procurer of material, and general organizer of a substantial building operation in an age which knew no labour exchanges, no builder's merchants, no quantity surveyors, and no professional architects. During the next few months he

[21] *Wren Society*, v (1928), 20, in a letter to the Bishop of Oxford.

[22] R. Willis and J. W. Clark, *Architectural History of the University of Cambridge*, ii (1886), 249.

was to spend a great deal of time on horseback, inspecting quarries, view-
ing standing timber, and arranging for the transport of both stone and
timber to Oxford.

After Hill's failure Lufton's first journey was to London 'to bargaine
with and gett new workemen of all sortes'.[23] With them came a new master mason, John Jackson. He eventually settled in Oxford, where he was
to carry out some important buildings, including the porch of St Mary's
Church, Brasenose Chapel and Library, and the upper part of the Cook's
Building at St John's.[24] What he had done before 1634 we do not know,
but he must have been recommended by someone who could vouch for
his competence. He was paid at the relatively high rate of 20*s.* a week for
supervising the masons' work, and himself executed some of the most
important sculpture.

Under Lufton's management the work now proceeded smoothly,
though he had a good deal of trouble in engaging and managing the
masons. One of the newcomers, Simon White by name, was immediately
sent to Chipping Campden in Gloucestershire (a place of which he was a
native) to engage more.[25] As a result of his efforts a contingent of Gloucestershire masons arrived in June.[26] Several of these 'would not come but at
extraordinary rates, which I yeelded to give them, but conceal'd from the
other workmen, according to whose rates Mr. Jackson payed them and I
made up the rest to them afterwards,' Lufton noted.[27] Every effort was
now made to make up for lost time: in August the masons' wages were
raised on the understanding that they would start at five in the morning
and work until seven at night, but in the next week they were each docked
2*d.* for drinks 'which they had out of the Buttery to keepe them from going
abroad'.[28] At the height of the summer there were about thirty masons at
work. The two frontispieces were by now well advanced, and in December
1634 the bronze statues of the King and Queen were set in place.[29]

The arcades on either side of the frontispieces were also complete. The
columns were made of a hard bluish-grey stone quarried at Bletchingdon,
five miles north-east of Woodstock and known as 'Bletchingdon marble'.
According to one report, this quarry had been discovered by President

[23] Building Accounts, p. 27.
[24] For his career see my *Biographical Dictionary of British Architects 1600–1840* (1978). For St
Mary's porch, see below, p. 119.
[25] Building Accounts, p. 26. For information
about Simon White I am indebted to Mrs J. C.
Cole.
[26] Some of them had to be compensated for
'leaving their work in the country', and Lufton
noted (p. 18) that four of them, headed by

Timothy Strong, were 'fech't out of my Lord
Da[n]vers's worcke beyond Burford', i.e. from
Cornbury Park, where they were working under
the direction of Nicholas Stone (see *The Note-
book and Account-book of Nicholas Stone*, ed. W.
L. Spiers, Walpole Society, vii (1918–19), p. 70).
[27] Building Accounts, p. 26.
[28] Ibid. 11–12.
[29] Ibid. 83, 'to Laborers helping to gett up the
Statues'.

Juxon himself while hunting in the neighbourhood.[30] The monolithic blocks had laboriously to be reduced to the correct size and then polished, the cracks and other blemishes being filled with a specially made cement. These defects ultimately proved fatal to several of the columns, which were replaced by Portland stone copies in 1905. The walls were built of a combination of Headington and Burford stone, the doorways, the windows, and other such features being of the latter material. The diagonally laid square paving-stones for the two cloister walks were of a hard limestone from Purbeck in Dorset, and were bought in London from 'hardstone men' whom Lufton spent some time searching out in City alehouses. From London they were transported by boat up the Thames as far as Burcot, near Abingdon, whence they were brought to Oxford on carts, some of them provided by the College's farm tenants at Long Wittenham. Unfortunately the purveyor of the Purbeck stone, one Moses Brampton, failed to send all that he had bargained to provide and the deficiency had to be made up with hardstone from the Bletchingdon quarry.[31]

The decorative carving that is such an important feature of the quadrangle was shared between Jackson and several specialist carvers. Jackson was personally responsible for the great shields displaying the arms of the King and Queen and of Archbishop Laud (as he had by now become), for certain other features of the two frontispieces, and for the sixteen symbolical busts or 'half-bodies', as they are called in the accounts, together with their attributes. The angels' heads in the upper frieze, the capitals and bases of the Ionic order, the decorative carving in the lower frieze, and the grotesques or 'anticks' in the string-courses were mainly carved by Harry Ackers and Anthony Gore. Gore was responsible for thirty-five of the forty-four sections of lower frieze, several of the angels' heads, the 'leather face' and festoons over the west cloister doorway, and for much of the architectural detail.[32] He and Ackers had both been employed by the London sculptor Nicholas Stone in 1632.[33] Others paid as stone-carvers at St John's were Ashbye, Bolton, Dominicus, Gravener, Larson, and the joiner Woodfield, who carved several angels and grotesques in the string-course.[34] The plumber who made the armorial 'cisterns' or rainwater-heads was James Fletcher.

[30] *Oxoniensia*, i (1936), 154.

[31] Building Accounts, pp. 51–2. Very little of the existing paving is of Purbeck stone.

[32] Ibid. esp. pp. 24–6 and 35. Jackson also carved the two heraldic shields over the new doorways in the Front Quadrangle (p. 60).

[33] *The Note-book and Account-book of Nicholas Stone*, pp. 34, 60, 89, 91. It might be supposed that Gore was the 'Anthony a Dutchman & workman to St. John Baptist Colledge—a stone carver', whose burial is recorded in the parish register of St. Giles' Church, Oxford, on 29 June 1635, but for the fact that, as Mr Adam White kindly informs me, there are several references to Anthony Gore as a freeman of the London Masons' Company during the years 1636–40.

[34] Building Accounts, pp. 20, 25, 26, 35.

7. Four of the carved keystones in the arches of the arcades. Despite their floral adornments the heads have no apparent iconographical significance.

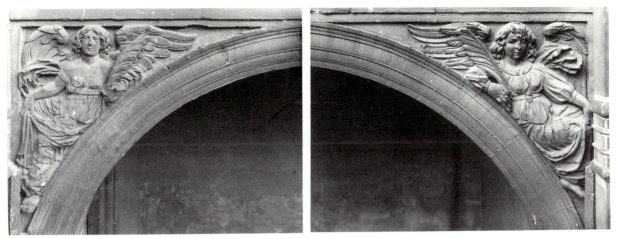

8. Two of the winged Victory figures carved in the end spandrels of the arcades

9. Two sections of the frieze above the arcade. The arms are those of William Laud

By the summer of 1635 the building was in its concluding stages, and in September, when the Court was at Woodstock, Laud took the opportunity to come over to give the final directions and distribute largesse to the workmen.[35] In October he formally handed the building over to the College, indicating the use to which the various parts should be put.[36] The gallery over the eastern cloister was to be an addition to the library, to house manuscripts, mathematical instruments and small books that could not easily be accommodated in the main library. The western gallery was to be for the use of the President, whose Lodgings had been enlarged and dignified by the addition of what is now known as the Great Parlour but was originally called the Great Chamber.[37] The ten new chambers in the north and south ranges were to be for the exclusive use of commoners, who, not being on the Foundation, were to pay for their accommodation, thus making a useful addition to the College's revenue.[38] These 'splendid rooms, the delight of gentlemen commoners' ('Generosorum Iuvenum deliciae Conclavia Augusta') are singled out for praise in Loggan's *Oxonia Illustra* of 1675.

On 26 March 1636 the account-book containing the record of Lufton's expenditure was formally delivered to Laud. The total cost of the quadrangle proved to be £5,553.[39] How Laud, whose revenues as Bishop of London were probably well below £2,000 a year, and whose income as Archbishop of Canterbury is unlikely to have exceeded £3,000,[40] was able to finance this expenditure is a matter for the ecclesiastical rather than the architectural historian, but there is no suggestion that the work was ever held up for lack of money. The latter reached the College in the form of regular remittances which varied from £20 to several hundreds at a time.[41] In 1631, in acknowledging Laud's intended benefaction, the fellows had politely observed that they would have supposed that his means 'were rather drained by domestic necessities than running over',[42] and three and a half centuries later we can only echo our predecessors' gratified surprise at Laud's financial resources.

Five months later Laud made his new quadrangle the setting for a grand entertainment of the King and Queen to celebrate the reforms and benefactions for which he had been responsible as Chancellor of the

---

[35] See Laud's Diary (*Works* iii, 224) and Building Accounts, p. 83.

[36] College Register, iii, 141.

[37] See below, pp. 80–3.

[38] See below, pp. 89–90.

[39] Building Accounts, p. 84.

[40] See F. Heal, *Of Prelates and Princes* (Cambridge, 1980), 272, 323, for some indication of

episcopal revenues.

[41] The receipts are among the State Papers Domestic in the PRO. See also p. 1 of the Building Accounts, listing the payments from Apr. 1633 onwards.

[42] PRO, SP 16/188, no. 66 ' . . . cum ex domesticis necessitatibus facultates tuas exhaustas magis credebamus quam superfluas . . . '.

University, and in particular the new Statutes which had just received royal approval. After inspecting the quadrangle the King and Queen were escorted to the new wing of the library, where they, the Elector Palatine, and Prince Rupert sat down to a dinner at which (to quote Anthony Wood) 'all the gallantry and beauties of the Kingdom seemed to meet'. The rest of the courtiers were accommodated at thirteen tables in various other parts of the College.[43] Vast quantities of provisions were consumed. Bucks, does, oxen, sheep, rabbits, capons, ducks, pheasants, turkeys, swans, and quails poured in, many as gifts from Laud's friends and supporters all over the country, from the King himself down to a Mistress Clarke (probably the wife of the College's under-cook)[44] who sent 'a cake and cream'.[45] Even so, the whole entertainment (including the play that followed) cost the astonishing sum of £2,666, equivalent to nearly half the cost of building the quadrangle.[46] The single most expensive item was the £540 paid to 'Mr. Sergeant Walthewe the King's Confectioner for the Banquet'. A banquet in the seventeenth century was a sort of dessert consisting of sweetmeats and wine, and for this occasion the confectioner modelled the entire hierarchy of the university: doctors, professors, canons, masters, and so forth, in paste and marzipan, so that, to quote a contemporary versifier, 'the ladies water'd ('bout the mouth) to see and tast so sweet a Universitie'.[47]

Such lavish entertainments had long been customary in connection with the installation of bishops and university chancellors, and this was just the sort of tradition that Laud would be anxious to maintain. As recently as 1632 the Earl of Holland had given 'a most Royal feast' to celebrate his installation as Chancellor of Cambridge University,[48] and many archbishops had done likewise on the occasion of their enthronement. One of the most elaborate archiepiscopal feasts was that given to mark the enthronement of William Warham as Archbishop of Canterbury in 1504, at which there was a whole series of gastronomic tableaux, showing for instance the University of Oxford, of which Warham was a Doctor and was soon, like Laud, to be Chancellor, presenting him to the King, the King presenting him to St Paul in his capacity as Master of the Rolls, and Saints Dunstan and Thomas presenting him to the Holy Trin-

[43] A. Wood, *History and Antiquities of the University of Oxford*, ed. J. Gutch ii/1 (1796), 410.

[44] Richard Clarke, the 'under-cook', had recently been given a lease of a house belonging to the College in consideration of his 'good and faithful services' (College Register, iii. 117).

[45] See the list of provisions in PRO, SP 16/348, no. 85.

[46] Ibid. 'The whole chardge of the Entertaynment cometh to £2666–1–7.'

[47] Edmund Gayton, *Epulae Oxonienses* (1661); *The Diary of Thomas Crosfield*, ed. F. S. Boas (1935), 93.

[48] PRO, Chancery Masters' Exhibits, C115/M.35/8397, newsletter dated 24 Mar. 1631/2.

ity as Archbishop of Canterbury.[49] These subtleties, as they were called, could therefore be serious as well as amusing in intention, and at St John's in 1636 there was another that, if correctly reported, ventured on very delicate ground indeed. It is described by a Scottish courtier, Sir David Cuningham of Auchenharvie, in a letter to a kinsman dated from Oatlands Palace on 4 October 1636. He wrote:

'I doubt not but you have heard ... of the extraordinarie entertainment and feasting made by the Bishop of Canterburie to the King and Queen at Oxford, where amongst many strange passages, the most remarkable was an invention of pyes walking, the one half representing English Bishops, with my lord's grace of Canterbury conducting them, th'other half forreign Cardinalls, with the Pope leading them, and both came to the King at table, one on his right hand and t'other on his left and were both received and made friends'.[50]

Even today such an ecumenical dessert would be likely to cause a considerable stir at a State Banquet, and in 1636, at a time when the Queen was a Catholic and Laud's High Church policies laid him open to accusations of popery, it must, as Cuningham wrote, have given rise to 'much talking and strange constructions'. It is hard to believe that Laud had approved of it in advance, and as no other reference to the incident has so far been found in contemporary sources, the accuracy of Cuningham's relation cannot be taken for granted. As a Presbyterian Scot wont (as his letters show) to deplore the extravagance of Charles I's court, he may have given his fellow-countryman an exaggerated account of the goings-on at Oxford. Nevertheless, as an important member of the Prince of Wales's household,[51] writing from a royal palace not long after the event his testimony cannot lightly be set aside. Precisely what happened in the newly finished library at St John's on 30 August 1636, and at whose instigation, may never be known. But it is not the least of the problems, both historical and architectural, to which the building of the Canterbury Quadrangle gives rise.

---

[49] See the account of the feast printed by Hearne as an appendix to his edition of Leland's *Collectanea*, vi (1715), 16–34.
[50] Scottish Record Office, GD237/221/4/1/54.

His correspondent was Sir David Cuningham of Robertland.
[51] G. E. Aylmer, *The King's Servants* (1961), 92, 320, 368–9.

2.

The Architecture of the Canterbury Quadrangle

THE feasting at St John's on 30 August 1636 was followed by a play in Christ Church hall for which Inigo Jones provided the setting.[1] We do not know whether the Surveyor of the King's Works was among the courtiers who were entertained by Laud on that summer's day, but we can hardly doubt that he took the opportunity to inspect this notable addition to Oxford's collegiate architecture. We can guess that what he saw, handsome though it was, would not have been much to his taste. Part Gothic, part Renaissance, part baroque, and none of it in the least Palladian, it represented a very different approach to architectural design from his own.

The arcades were of the early Renaissance type, without half-columns or pilasters to support the entablature, and with arches springing directly from the capitals, not the proper Roman kind derived from such ancient exemplars as the Theatre of Marcellus (Fig. 10). From its proportions the order was apparently Tuscan, but in the frieze above Doric triglyphs could be seen scattered about in a way that defied all Vitruvian rule or Palladian precept. In the centre the fluted Doric order, to be sure, derived from some reasonably respectable source such as Vignola, but higher up the twin Ionic columns stood on unorthodox double pedestals, themselves covered with meretricious ornament of Flemish extraction, while the pediment they supported was not of a kind illustrated by the authorities that Jones respected. And on either side there were the Tudor Gothic windows and battlements, totally at variance with both arcades and frontispieces, while to get into the quadrangle or out of it one had to pass under fan-vaulted passageways (Figs. 11–12) framed by doorways full of 'leather faces' and other mannerist conceits (Figs. 13–14).

It was emphatically not the kind of building that Jones would have sanctioned, had he been consulted, but however incongruous the mixture of Gothic and classic may have seemed to him in 1636 and must seem to ourselves today, it would not necessarily have incurred general censure in the reign of Charles I. In Paris there were churches like St Eustache and St Etienne-du-Mont where the clash of styles seems to have been quite

[1] S. Orgel and R. Strong, *Inigo Jones: The Theatre of the Stuart Court* (1975), 823.

10. The north-east
corner of the
Canterbury
Quadrangle

11. The fan-
vaulted roof of the
passageway
between the
Canterbury
Quadrangle and
the garden

12. The fan-vaulted roof of the passageway between the Front Quadrangle and the Canterbury Quadrangle

13. Detail of the archway on the west side of the Canterbury Quadrangle

14. The archway on the east side of the Canterbury Quandrangle

deliberate, while in England the church of St Katherine Cree in London (1628–31) and the chapel and library of Brasenose College (begun in 1656) are examples of buildings where Gothic and classical features are combined in a way that cannot be attributed to mere inadvertence and which suggests a sophisticated delight in the unlikely combination of theoretically incompatible elements. Another is the porch of the University church of St Mary, built in 1637 by one of Laud's protégés, and closely connected stylistically with his own work at St John's.[2]

In the Canterbury Quadrangle it was of course the pre-existence of the Tudor Gothic library which made a completely classical quadrangle impossible, while a completely Gothic one would have seemed unduly old-fashioned to anyone as closely associated with the Court of Charles I as Laud. In any case the introduction of classical arcading into a traditional architectural setting, though an innovation in Oxford, was by no means without precedent in English architecture. In a European context, arcades of this sort go back to Brunelleschi and the Florentine Renaissance. In England an early example can be seen in the courtyard of Burghley House in Northamptonshire, built by William Cecil, Queen Elizabeth's Secretary of State, in the 1550s, where the arcading is combined with a gateway decorated with superimposed orders of classical columns (Fig. 15). But to a courtier like Laud the most familiar examples were probably at Cecil's other great mansion, Theobalds in Hertfordshire, built between 1567 and 1574 and since 1607 a royal residence; at Hatfield House, built by Robert Cecil in 1607–11; the Royal Exchange in London (1566–70) (Fig. 16); and the Queen's London palace, Somerset House in the Strand, where the arcading dated from 1611–12 (Fig. 17). There was also the example of Neville's Court at Trinity College, Cambridge, built in 1605–12.[3]

Although there were no such arcades in Oxford, superimposed orders had been used in the recent past at Merton and Wadham, and most conspicuously in the Schools, in order to dignify the sides of quadrangles, so it was a logical step to introduce the complementary arcading already so familiar from the great courtiers' houses. That was what happened at St John's in 1632 at the behest of the greatest courtier of them all.

If, however, we turn to the two frontispieces, we find ourselves confronted with something rather different in style and scale from the superimposed orders of Merton or the Schools Quadrangle, whose columns (to

[2] See below, p. 119.
[3] For Theobalds see J. Summerson, 'The Building of Theobalds, 1564–1585', *Archaeologia*, 97 (1959); for the Royal Exchange, engravings reproduced in A. M. Hind, *Wenceslas Hollar and his Views of London* (1922), pl. xxxii; and for Somerset House, *History of the King's Works*, ed. H. M. Colvin, iv (1982), 258.

A Perspective View of the inner Court of Burghley House taken from the West End under the Arch near the Golden Gates. By I. Haynes A.D MDCCLV.

15. The arcade in the courtyard at Burghley House, North-amptonshire, built in the 1550s, from a drawing dated 1755 (*Country Life*)

16. The Royal Exchange, London, built 1566–70, from an engraving by W. Hollar dated 1644 (Ashmolean Museum, Oxford, Sutherland Collection)

17. Old Somerset House, London, showing the arcade built 1611–12, from an 18th-century engraving (Bodleian Library, Oxford, Gough maps 22, fo. 53ᵛ)

quote a contemporary critic) look like things 'patcht or glewed against a wall' (Fig. 18).[4] Indeed these gauche experiments with the orders compare very ill with some French examples—for instance the mid-sixteenth-century elevations of the Louvre, where the projecting frontispieces form part of a coherent architectural design—and make it painfully obvious that there can have been little real understanding of classical architecture among either those who designed them or those who commissioned them.

But the St John's frontispieces, despite their semi-Gothic setting, are more sophisticated affairs: they are bolder, more grandiloquent; in fact they are not retarded Renaissance, like the arcades, but baroque. Nothing quite like them had been seen in England before, and to find their prototypes we have to go to Northern France and the Southern Netherlands. Ultimately, of course, nearly every feature has an Italian origin, but the immediate source proves to be French or Flemish.

If we take the pediment that crowns the whole composition we find that the ultimate prototype is a frame for a papal statue added to the front of the Palazzo Comunale at Bologna by the architect Tibaldi in 1580 (Fig. 19). But this type of shallow curved pediment with a solid

---

[4] Sir Balthazar Gerbier, *A Brief Discourse of Magnificent Building* (1662), 4.

18. Superimposed orders at (*left*) Merton and (*right*) Wadham College, Oxford, both built in 1610–11. At Merton the pediment was originally flanked by pairs of finials

segment at each end supported by coupled columns was a feature of French church façades in the early seventeenth century. In Paris St Gervais (1616) and the church of the Feuillants (1623) were well-known examples, and the ones most likely to have been familiar to the designer of the Oxford frontispieces (Fig. 20).

If we take the curious motif on the pedestals of the Doric order of an animal's skin stretched out with its head and feet hanging down (Fig. 21), we find this in an engraving made in Antwerp from a drawing by Rubens, though Rubens got the idea from the Italian artist and engraver Tempesta. Tempesta had used it, appropriately enough, for the dedication of a suite of hunting prints, published in Rome in 1605 (Fig. 23). Rubens adapted it for the title-page of a collection of engravings for the teaching of drawing which he published in the late 1620s, the ox being the symbol of St Luke, the patron saint of artists (Fig. 22).[5] Here at St John's the skins are apparently those of lions and may therefore be intended as symbols of royalty, though if so their significance is not as obvious as that of the lions' masks that form corbels beneath the statues of the King and Queen.

The pedestals of the Ionic order are based on Roman altars with rams' heads at the corners (Fig. 25). The source for this is a French architectural textbook by Philibert de l'Orme, first published in Paris in 1567 (Fig. 24), but this too has its reflection in certain Netherlandish engravings, including a title-page designed by Rubens for a book published in Antwerp in 1618.[6]

The pervasive influence of Rubens—at this time the dominant figure in the artistic life of Antwerp, itself until recently the commercial centre of Northern Europe—is probably also to be seen in two other features of the quadrangle.

One is the heads of angels or cherubs that decorate the friezes. Such heads are often to be found in friezes from the Renaissance onwards, but they are particularly prominent in the Jesuit Church in Antwerp, a much-admired building which was sumptuously decorated in about 1620 under Rubens's personal direction.[7] In the Canterbury Quadrangle, as in the church, they are sometimes attractively animated by looking to one side instead of being mere expressionless masks staring straight ahead (Fig. 26).

[5] M. Rooses, *L'Œuvre de P. P. Rubens*, v (Antwerp, 1892), 24. Another version of this motif as used for the title-page of a book published in Prague in 1606 is illustrated by J. R. Judson and C. van de Velde, Corpus Rubenianum Ludwig Burchard, 21 (1978), fig. 201.

[6] Illustrated ibid., fig. 148. For other examples of this motif prior to 1635 see *Hendrik Goltzius: The Complete Engravings and Woodcuts*, ed. W. L. Strauss (New York, 1977), pl. 168 (dated 1583); Villamena's engraved portrait of Inigo Jones, c.1614 (*The King's Arcadia: Inigo Jones and the Stuart Court*, ed. J. Harris, S. Orgel, and R. Strong (1973), fig. 406); and Van Dyck's portrait of George Gage in the National Gallery (c.1622/3).

[7] A. Blunt, 'Rubens and Architecture', *Burlington Magazine*, 119 (1977), 617.

19. Bologna, the Palazzo Comunale, showing the Ionic order and segmental pediment framing the statue of Pope Gregory XIII and designed by Domenico Tibaldi, 1580

20. Facade of the church of St Gervais, Paris, designed by Salomon de Brosse, 1616 (from a contemporary engraving)

21. Pedestal of Doric order, with carved representation of lion's skin

22. Title-page designed by Rubens *c.*1625–30 with engraved representation of ox's skin (Bodleian Library, Oxford, Douce Prints W.21 (308))

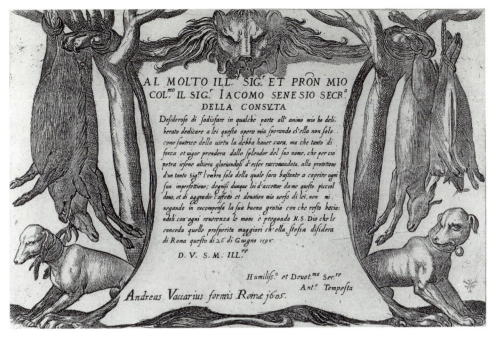

23. Title-page for suite of hunting prints designed by Antonio Tempesta, 1605 (Ashmolean Museum, Oxford, small Talman album)

The other is the heraldic beasts—a lion and a unicorn—which crouch rather uncomfortably beneath the pediments that shelter the two royal statues (Fig. 34). Usually such beasts were shown standing in silhouette on either side of a coat of arms. But two lions were placed in exactly the same posture on one of the triumphal arches designed by Rubens for the ceremonial entry of the Cardinal Infante Ferdinand into Antwerp in 1635 (Fig. 27). Now the decision to construct the arches was not taken until November 1634, and Rubens was hard at work on their design in December.[8] At Oxford the lions and unicorns had already been 'bosted out' by then and must have been finished by 12 December, when the bronze statues were hauled up into place.[9] So in this detail the Canterbury Quadrangle was actually slightly ahead of Rubens's latest work in Antwerp.

Finally, to remove any doubt as to the Netherlandish affinities of much of the architectural decoration of the Canterbury Quadrangle, the gateway to the garden is taken directly from a book of architectural engravings published in Brussels in 1617 by the Flemish architect Jacques

[8] J. R. Martin, *The Decorations for the Pompa Introitus Ferdinandi* (Corpus Rubenianum Ludwig Burchard, 16 (1972)), pp. 24–6; E. McGrath, 'Le Déclin d'Anvers et les décorations de Rubens pour l'entrée du prince Ferdinand en 1635', in *Les Fêtes de la Renaissance*, ed. J. Jacquot and E. Konigson, iii (1975).

[9] Building Accounts, pp. 25, 83.

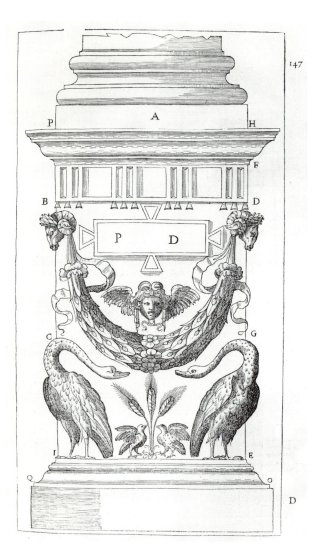

147

24. Design for pedestal of Doric order, from Philibert de l'Orme, *Le premier tome de l'Architecture* (1567)

25. Double pedestal of Ionic order, Canterbury Quadrangle

26. *Above*. Frieze of confessional in Chapel of N. Dame in Jesuit Church, Antwerp, showing one of the winged cherubs' heads which are a feature of the decoration of this church, carried out under the direction of Rubens *c.*1620. *Below*. Winged cherubs' heads in the frieze of the Ionic order, Canterbury Quadrangle, photographed in 1907

27. Engraving of triumphal arch designed by Rubens and erected in Antwerp in 1635. Compare the lion and unicorn in Fig. 34. (From *Pompa Introitus Serenissimi Principis Ferdinandi Austriaci Hispaniarum Infantis . . . MDCXXXV . . . Arcus, Pegmata, iconesque a Pet. Paulo Rubenio, Equite, inventis & delineatis . . .* , Antwerp, 1641–2 (Bodleian Library, Oxford, Mason S. 212, p. 28))

28. *Left*. Design for gateway from Jacques Francart's *Premier livre d'Architecture* (Brussels, 1617). *Right*. Garden gateway, Canterbury Quadrangle

Francart (Fig. 28). Clearly, then, someone with a knowledge of French and Netherlandish architecture must have had a hand in designing the quadrangle.

Now the most unorthodox feature of the whole composition is the two-tiered pedestal on which the Ionic order stands. Double pedestals of this sort are most unusual, though they are occasionally found in altar-pieces. It rather looks as if there was a space to be filled up, and this in turn suggests that the upper part of the frontispieces represents a revised design.

29. Elevation of the east side of the Canterbury Quadrangle, from a drawing by F.W. Troup, 1888 (St John's College Muniments, lxxxii. 38)

There is in fact evidence that the frontispieces as we see them today were designed after work on the arcades was well advanced. In Lufton's accounts they are always called 'fronts'[10] and in January 1633 he paid 6*d*. 'for carriage of the boxe that brought downe the drafts of the fronts' and 12*d*. 'for carriage of it back to London'. Then in February paper was brought 'to draw the Molds' and a Mr Browne was paid £5 'for his paines in comming downe & drawing the Drafts and making the Moulds'.[11] It is a reasonable inference that these drafts were working drawings for the frontispieces, and as the frontispieces were of course designed to accommodate the two royal statues it is worth noting that it was on 2 May 1633 that the agreement for making the latter was signed by the sculptor.[12] The successive failures of Maude and Hill to fulfil their contracts meant that work on the frontispieces was not in fact carried out until 1634, by which time the heraldry had been revised to take account of Laud's translation to Canterbury.

But if the existing frontispieces were not designed until 1633, are we to suppose that when the masons began work on their new contract in 1632 they had no idea what the frontispieces were to be like? No, because it is evident from both structural and documentary evidence that the lower stage of the frontispieces is integral with the arcades, and was in fact built with them, before the upper part.[13] In 1632 those concerned must have envisaged the upper stage which the paired Doric columns were intended to support, and we can guess what it might have looked like if we compare the lower stage of the Canterbury Quadrangle frontispieces with the lower stages of the frontispieces of other early seventeenth-century buildings, domestic or collegiate, that were similarly adorned (Figs. 30, 31). What we find is almost invariably an order of coupled Doric columns similar to those in the Canterbury Quadrangle, and above it further orders of Ionic, Corinthian, and sometimes Composite, columns. At the top there is a more or less fanciful termination, sometimes incorporating a pediment.[14] If we apply such an arrangement to the Canterbury Quadrangle with suitable adjustments it would just fit the available space and provide a frame for a statue and a coat of arms, as at Merton and Wadham (Fig. 32).

A decision to scrap some hackneyed design of this sort in favour of a

---

[10] Ibid. 6, 22, 25, 47 (*bis*), 61v, 64 (*bis*).

[11] Ibid. 81.

[12] SP 16/238, fos. 16–17 (below, p. 117).

[13] The four pedestals with the lions' skins were carved later by Jackson to bring them into harmony with the upper parts of the frontispieces, as recorded in the Building Accounts, p. 35.

[14] Illustrations of several examples will be found in J. A. Gotch's *Architecture of the Renaissance in England* (1891–5). For Beaupré Hall in Glamorganshire see Royal Commission on Historical Monuments in Wales, *Glamorgan*, 4 (1981), figs. 1 and 6.

30. Audley End, Essex, the south side of the Great Court, as represented in an engraving by Henry Winstanley, 1688 (Bodleian Library, Oxford, Gough Maps 8, fo.58^r)

31. Beaupré Hall, Glamorganshire, the Jacobean porch (National Monuments Record for Wales)

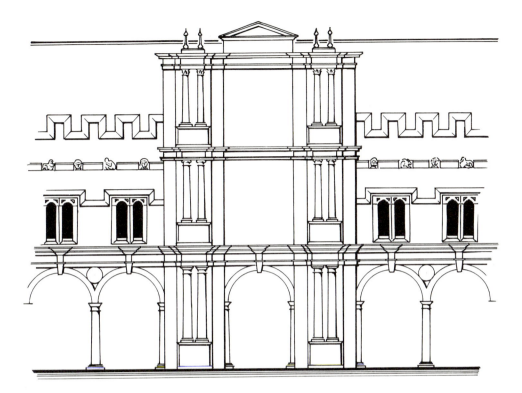

32. Conjectural drawing showing the form in which the St John's frontispieces may originally have been envisaged, with two further orders of coupled columns above the Doric order

33. Gateway at St Catharine's College, Cambridge, built 1674–9

34. The bronze statues of King Charles I and Queen Henrietta Maria, by Hubert Le Sueur (*Sir John Kendrew*)

bolder baroque composition would have meant that one order had to take the place of two: and as the Ionic columns could not be stretched sufficiently to fill the space, the double pedestal was the answer. When a baroque gateway was designed *de novo* this difficulty was avoided by raising the lower story above first-floor level to form a plinth for the upper order, as for instance at Clare and St Catharine's Colleges in Cambridge (Fig. 33). At St John's the double plinth is the only tell-tale sign of a transformation so skillfully accomplished that few notice that the upper part of the frontispiece is not quite homogeneous with the lower.

Before considering who might have been responsible for this transformation it is necessary to look at the decorative features of the quadrangle, particularly the two bronze statues of Charles I and his Queen (Fig. 34). They were the work of Hubert Le Sueur, a French Huguenot sculptor who had come to England in 1624 or 1625 and was much employed by Charles I and the Court circle.[15] Today his best-known work is the statue of Charles I on horseback at Charing Cross. Le Sueur was the son of an armourer and his knowledge of armour was better than his knowledge of anatomy. His figures lack subtlety in modelling and show more interest in dress than in facial expression. But as symbols of royalty to be seen at a respectful distance the two statues commissioned by Laud for the Canterbury Quadrangle splendidly fulfil their hieratic function. When Oxford surrendered to the Parliamentary forces in 1646, they must have been seriously at risk. According to one tradition they were taken down and buried to save them from destruction; according to another they were offered for sale by the Parliamentary authorities, but 'were ignorantly refused, because not solid' and so survived, to be reinstated at the Restoration.[16]

Then there is the series of busts in the roundels above the columns of the arcades, attractive but less-accomplished works, all supplied and presumably carved by the master mason Jackson. On the west side these represent Virtues, on the east the Liberal Arts. As there were only seven canonical virtues—Faith, Hope, Charity, Prudence, Justice, Fortitude, and Temperance—but eight roundels to fill, an extra bust representing Religion was added. In the same way on the other side Astronomy, Geometry, Music, Arithmetic, Logic, Rhetoric, and Grammar were supplemented by Learning to fill the extra space.

Representations of the Liberal Arts had long been regarded as an appropriate decoration for a library, and there was an equally long iconographical tradition which associated them with the seven Virtues.[17] There

---

[15] For Le Sueur see G. Webb, 'Notes on Hubert le Sueur', *Burlington Magazine*, 52 (1928), 10, 81 and C. Avery, 'Hubert le Sueur', *Walpole Society*, xlviii (1980–2). The contract with Le Sueur is printed in Appendix V.

[16] A. Wood, *The History of the Colleges and Halls in the University of Oxford* (1674), ed. J. Gutch (1786), p. 548, n. 46.

[17] A. Masson, *Le Décor des bibliothèques du Moyen Âge à la Révolution* (Paris, 1972), 48 ff.

were, for instance, inscriptions naming both Arts and Virtues on the walls of the medieval Schools of Arts in Oxford before the present Schools were built.[18] But by the seventeenth century other themes inspired by Humanist ideals or Counter-Reformation theology were generally thought more suitable for the decoration of libraries, and the display of Liberal Arts and Virtues in the Canterbury Quadrangle must be seen as one more manifestation of what Sir Richard Southern has called 'Laud's sustained attempt to restore the medieval system of thought in almost every department of theology, philosophy and science'.[19]

The Virtues are quite easy to recognize by their long-established symbols: Hope with her anchor, Justice with her sword, Temperance mixing wine with water, and so forth. The Arts are accompanied by suitable instruments and often by books bearing the titles of appropriate authorities (Fig. 35). Here is Rhetoric with the works of Demosthenes, Cicero, Hermogenes, and Quintilian, here is Geometry not only accompanied by Euclid and Archimedes but also by Vitruvius, the principal classical authority on architecture, and literally wearing the hat of Architecture—still of course officially regarded as a Mechanical Art and therefore inadmissible in her own right (Fig. 36).

Although the scheme of Arts and Virtues was therefore thoroughly conventional, not to say old-fashioned, its actual representation was a little unusual in that the personifications are merely busts, with their symbols carved on either side of them. Elsewhere they were normally shown as figures holding or wielding their respective symbols. In a contemporary engraving, for instance, we see Temperance mixing water with wine. But in the Canterbury Quadrangle an unseen hand performs this symbolic act on either side of a complacent bust (Fig. 37). Now it was an established convention going back to Antiquity to decorate arcades with roundels and for these roundels to contain busts, often of Roman Emperors or other classical personages. What we have in the Canterbury Quadrangle is therefore the fusion of two iconographical traditions, the bust in the roundel and the personification of the Arts and Virtues.

Finally there is the ubiquitous heraldry, displayed on the small shields in the lower frieze, by larger ones held by angels in the Gothic string-courses, and by the huge shields which depend from the frontispieces (Fig. 38). In an age which took heraldry seriously the placing of the royal arms high above those of the archbishop might be understood to indicate Laud's loyal acceptance of the Royal Supremacy. But on the splendid lead rainwater heads (Fig. 39) the alternation of crown and mitre would no

---

[18] N. Chytraeus, *Variorum in Europa Itinerum Deliciae* (Herborn, 1599), 598–9.

[19] In an unpublished lecture on Laud from which he has kindly allowed me to quote.

35. Bust representing Grammar, flanked by keys and appropriately titled books (see p. 110)

36. Bust representing Geometry, wearing a mural crown symbolizing Architecture, and flanked by architectural tools and instruments (see p. 109)

37. *Above*. Engraving by Crispin de Passe (1600) representing Temperance mixing water with wine (Victoria and Albert Museum Print Room). *Below*. Bust representing Temperance (see p. 108)

38. The arms of Archbishop Laud in the western frontispiece, photographed in 1907

39. Lead rainwater heads bearing the arms of King Charles I and Archbishop Laud

doubt symbolize that interdependence of Church and State which was at the heart of Laud's political philosophy.

It remains to consider the problem that underlies the whole of this discussion: who designed the Canterbury Quadrangle? It is hardly necessary to insist on the improbability of the old attribution to Inigo Jones, which is now more of an art-historical curiosity than something that needs serious refutation.[20] A more pertinent question is: why did Laud not employ Jones? As a leading member of the Court he could surely have commanded Jones's services—indeed he had already done so in connection with the repair of his own cathedral church of St Paul in London. Moreover, as a member of the Privy Council he saw a good deal of Jones as the agent of the Commissioners for regulating building in London. It might be tempting to speculate that it was the realization by one masterful man that he and the equally masterful Jones were not likely to agree.

But the answer lies rather in the history of the building. Had the Canterbury Quadrangle been a complete new building on a virgin site, then Jones might have been a suitable architect. But as we have seen, its construction and design were a piecemeal process. The north wing that Laud originally commissioned to match the existing library needed no architect. The master mason Maude was perfectly capable of reproducing the south side of the quadrangle on the north, and of adding to the north elevation (Fig. 40) some of those mannerist gables that he was later to employ at University College and in the second quadrangle at Jesus.[21] Indeed the making of 'drafts' and 'modells' was one of the services for which he and his partners claimed remuneration in 1633.[22]

When the classical arcades were under consideration early in 1632, the general idea may have been Laud's, but it is clear from their correspondence that he left it to Juxon to work out the details on the spot. The design was evidently embodied in the model made by the joiner Woodfield.[23] This model may have been based on drawings made by Maude as the head of the new consortium of mason-contractors which was to carry it out, but a more likely candidate is his partner Hugh Davies. In the 1620s Davies had for a time been employed as a mason at Whitehall

---

[20] Though much more plausible, Arthur Oswald's suggestion that the London master mason Nicholas Stone might have been the designer (*Country Life*, 66 (9 Nov. 1929)) must be rejected. Had Stone been involved in the design of the Quadrangle, it is hardly conceivable that he would not have been mentioned in the building accounts, and he rather than Adam Browne would surely have 'drawn the drafts and made the moulds' in 1633. It should also be noted that the Canterbury Quadrangle does not figure either in the list of his works drawn up by his nephew Charles Stoakes, or in his own Account-book (ed. W. L. Spiers, *Walpole Society*, vii (1918–19)).

[21] *Victoria County History of Oxfordshire*, iv. 75, 274.

[22] PRO, SP 16/254, fo. 16.

[23] Building Accounts, p. 65: 'For the Modell'. It took thirty-one days to make and Woodfield's bill included 18*d*. 'for turning the Pillers'. On 1 June 1632 12*d*. was spent on 'bringing the Modell from Woodfeilds to the Lodgings' (p. 81).

40. The exterior of the Canterbury Quadrangle, as seen from the north

under Inigo Jones;[24] then in 1632–4 he was concerned in the design for the western extension of the Bodleian Library, and made a 'great model' for a projected staircase which he took up to London to show to Laud as Chancellor. In the event nothing came of this, but in a document connected with his remuneration Davies is described as 'Architector'.[25] So Davies could well have been the man who designed the arcades and the old-fashioned frontispieces which I have suggested were originally intended to go with them.

Then in January 1633 there was the arrival from London of 'the boxe that brought downe the drafts of the fronts'. Soon afterwards Lufton paid £5 to 'Mr. Browne for his paines in comming downe and drawing the drafts and making the Moulds'.[26] If I am right these would be the working drawings for the upper parts of the two frontispieces.

So who was Mr Browne? Adam Browne was a master joiner by trade, and in that capacity was much employed by Laud. In 1633 he made an altar and other joinery work for Laud at Lambeth, and in 1632 he had made a screen in the chapel at St John's at Laud's expense.[27] At Laud's trial he was a reluctant witness, giving evidence about allegedly 'Popish' windows ordered by Laud for his houses at Lambeth and Croydon and

[24] PRO, Account of the Paymaster of the Works 1625–6 (E 351/3259).
[25] I. G. Philip, 'The Building of the Schools Quadrangle', *Oxoniensia*, xiii (1948), 47–8; Oxford University Archives WP β 5 (5).
[26] Building Accounts, p. 81.
[27] PRO, SP 16/246, no. 88; SP 16/226, fo. 21.

put up under Browne's direction.[28] Like other master workmen he was
capable of acting as an architect or surveyor and in 1639 he was
appointed Surveyor to Westminster Abbey.[29] Two surviving works give
us some idea of his capacity as a designer and craftsman. One is the chimney-piece in the Jerusalem Chamber at Westminster Abbey (Fig. 41), the
other a cabinet at Arbury Hall, Warwickshire, which bears Laud's arms
as Bishop of London, and must therefore have been made for him
between 1628 and 1633 (Fig. 42). It is so similar in style to the chimney-
piece that there can be little doubt that it too was Browne's work. Both
are in a mannerist style ultimately Flemish in derivation but not at all
close to that of the Canterbury Quadrangle frontispieces. We may conjec-
ture that between 1629, when he made the chimney-piece for the Jerusalem Chamber,[30] and 1633, when he was making drawings for the
Canterbury Quadrangle, Browne was exposed to fresh artistic influences,
but by what means or at whose instigation we do not know. There is a
gap here in our evidence which only speculation can fill. Some ninety
years ago Sir Reginald Blomfield, in the course of a remarkably perspi-
cacious paragraph about the Canterbury Quadrangle in his *History of
Renaissance Architecture in England* (1897), suggested that the frontispieces might have been designed by Hubert Le Sueur, the sculptor whose
workmanship they frame, or by some other 'foreign artist about the
court', and this is a possibility that deserves serious consideration.

There are indeed some features which the architecture of the Canterbury Quadrangle shares with a small group of prestigious monuments
made for leading members of the Court of Charles I, monuments which
have long been attributed to Le Sueur. One of these is the monument to
the Duke of Richmond and Lennox in Westminster Abbey, completed by
1628 (Fig. 43), where we find the same S-curved broken pediment as we
do on the doorway that leads into the Canterbury Quadrangle from the
Front Quadrangle (Fig. 44)—later a standard baroque motif that at this
date was still relatively unusual either in England or in France.[31] This part
of the monument is carved in black marble, but above on the cornice there
are four bronze urns decorated with rams' heads like the ones on the
pedestals of the Ionic order in the Canterbury Quadrangle. Rams' heads
carved in marble also occur both on the monument to the Duke of Buckingham in Westminster Abbey, under construction in the early 1630s, and

[28] W. Prynne, *A complete History of the Tryall
. . . of William Laud, late Archbishop of Canterbury* (1646), 61; Laud, *Works*, ed. Bliss, iv, 209,
228.
[29] H. Colvin, *Biographical Dictionary of*

British Architects 1600–1840 (1978), 149–50.
[30] Westminster Abbey Muniments 6612. I owe
this reference to Dr Christopher Wilson.
[31] A. Blunt, *Baroque and Rococo* (1978), 146.

42. Cabinet at Arbury Hall, Warwickshire, bearing Laud's arms as Bishop of London (*Country Life*)

41. Chimney-piece in the Jerusalem Chamber at Westminster Abbey, made by Adam Browne in 1629 (*Royal Commission on the Historical Monuments of England*)

on that of Lord Treasurer Weston in Winchester Cathedral, commissioned during his lifetime and completed before his death in 1635. There is some doubt whether Le Sueur was responsible for the bronze effigy of Weston, and in any case there is evidence that the marble sculpture on this tomb and probably also on that of the Duke of Buckingham was the work of Isaac Besnier, who was to succeed Le Sueur as Sculptor to Charles I when Le Sueur left England in 1643.[32] If Weston's effigy was not Le Sueur's work then it must almost certainly have been made by the Italian sculptor Francesco Fanelli, the only other artist at Charles I's court capable of casting in bronze. It is to Fanelli that students of English sculpture have generally attributed another courtier's monument in Westminster Abbey, that of Sir Robert Ayton, who died in 1638,[33] and on that monument we find two of the motifs that we have been pursuing united, for the epitaph is inscribed on a stretched-out animal's skin with the head neither of a lion nor an ox, but of a ram (Fig. 45).

So here we have three Court sculptors—Le Sueur, Besnier, and Fanelli—all of whom were using motifs that appear in the Canterbury Quadrangle. If, like Sir Reginald Blomfield, we see the frontispieces as 'essentially sculptor's work', in which decoration is paramount, then we may conclude that they could have been designed by one of these sculptors, and of the three Le Sueur is obviously the most likely. However, Le Sueur, like Fanelli, was a specialist in bronze and it is doubtful whether he made designs for execution by others in stone or marble. Nor does the fact that the sculptor and the designer of the frontispieces shared some motifs prove that they were the same person—only that they had access to the same artistic source.

As has been shown, several of these motifs can be traced to the Netherlands, and in particular to Antwerp, where Rubens was the presiding artistic genius. Rubens himself had of course been in England on a diplomatic mission in 1629 and he subsequently painted the ceiling of the Banqueting House at Whitehall, with its baroque apotheosis of James I. But although Rubens did design a handful of funeral monuments in Flanders,[34] it is most unlikely that he designed any for English patrons, still less that he had anything to do with the Canterbury Quadrangle. Was there anyone who might have acted as a link between the Antwerp of Rubens and the Court of Charles I?

There was a man who fulfilled precisely that role. His name was Sir Balthazar Gerbier, and since 1631 he had been Charles I's resident agent

[32] Letter from Besnier to Gerbier dated 7/17 Feb. 1632, in PRO, SP 77/21, no. 69 (fo. 52).

[33] L. Cust in *DNB*, s.v. 'Fanelli': M. Whinney, *Sculpture in England 1530–1830* (1964), 37, and

C. Avery, 'Hubert le Sueur', *Walpole Society*, xlviii (1980–2), 191.

[34] J. S. Held, 'Rubens' designs for Monuments', *Art Quarterly*, 23 (1960).

43. Westminster Abbey, monument to the Duke of Richmond and Lennox (d. 1624), from an engraving in J. Dart's *Westmonasterium* (1742)

44. Entrance to Canterbury Quadrangle from Front Quadrangle, with Laud's arms

45. Westminster Abbey, monument to Sir Robert Ayton (d. 1638), with bronze bust and epitaph inscribed on a representation of an animal's skin with a ram's head (*Royal Commission on the Historical Monuments of England*)

in Brussels. The child of French Protestant parents, he had been born in the Netherlands and had come to England in 1616. His training was probably as a calligraphic artist, but besides 'a good hand in writing' he laid claim to 'skill in science as mathematics, architecture, drawing, painting, contriving of scenes, masques, shows and entertainments for great princes' as well as military engineering.[35] Moreover, he was an astute art-dealer and in that capacity had built up a magnificent collection of paintings and other works of art for his patron the Duke of Buckingham, who also employed him to paint miniatures and to embellish his houses.[36] As Charles I's agent in Brussels Gerbier's duties were mainly diplomatic, but he bought pictures for his royal master and also for the Earl of Arundel.[37] Both as an artist and as a diplomat he was in constant touch with Rubens, and when Rubens came to London in 1629 it was Gerbier who acted as his host. Gerbier also knew Le Sueur (a fellow Huguenot), whose equestrian statue of Charles I was the centre-piece of the garden he designed for Lord Treasurer Weston at Roehampton,[38] and when Weston commissioned his monument in Winchester Cathedral, Besnier sent Gerbier a sketch of the design.[39] In 1634 Gerbier's services as a cultural go-between were exercised on behalf of Archbishop Laud himself. Laud experienced difficulty in procuring the types necessary to achieve one of his favourite schemes, the setting up of a Greek press in London. With the help of Rubens Gerbier went to Antwerp in person to secure the necessary founts.[40]

As a practising architect Gerbier has left few traces: of his work for the Duke of Buckingham only the York House watergate survives as probably his design;[41] of Weston's house at Roehampton only the statue of Charles I; and of the great mansion which he began for Lord Craven at Hamstead Marshall virtually nothing at all. In one signed drawing for Hamstead Marshall (Fig. 46) and two portraits drawn by Gerbier we see leathery cartouches of the sort that are so prominent a feature of the frontispieces in the Canterbury Quadrangle.[42] Too much must not be made of

[35] For Gerbier's career see *DNB* and H. Ross Williamson, *Four Stuart Portraits* (1949).

[36] I. G. Philip, 'Balthazar Gerbier and the Duke of Buckingham's Pictures', *Burlington Magazine*, 99 (1957), 155–6; L. R. Betcherman, 'The York House Collection and its Keeper', *Apollo*, 92 (1970).

[37] See Gerbier's entry-books of his correspondence in PRO, SP 105/7–18, *passim*.

[38] For Gerbier as Weston's architect and artistic adviser see PRO, SP 16/153/69, SP 16/158, 48, 54, SP 77/21/221, SP 105/8, fos. 26–7.

[39] PRO, SP 77/21, no. 69 (fo. 52).

[40] W. N. Sainsbury, *Original Papers Illustrative of the Life of Sir Peter Paul Rubens* (1859), 187; H. R. Trevor-Roper, *Archbishop Laud* (1962), 275.

[41] J. Summerson, *Architecture in Britain 1530–1830* (1953), 85. This attribution is by no means certain.

[42] The drawing is reproduced in *Architectural Drawings in the Bodleian Library* (1952), pl. 2. For the portraits see E. Croft-Murray and P. Hilton, *Catalogue of British Drawings in the British Museum* (1960), pls. 133–4.

these: such cartouches were a commonplace of European sculptural decoration in the 1630s. But if we are looking for someone who could have
provided—or been instrumental in obtaining—a drawing for the frontispieces which Adam Browne was subsequently employed to work out in
detail, then Gerbier is an obvious candidate.

Unfortunately no reference to the Canterbury Quadrangle can be
found in Gerbier's extant correspondence.[43] It is true that the correspondence is largely of an official character, consisting of diplomatic des-
patches to the King and his ministers, and many other letters have
doubtless been lost. Nevertheless, in the absence of any scrap of docu-
mentation, Gerbier's possible involvement in the design of the Canterbury Quadrangle must remain an unsubstantiated hypothesis until some
further piece of evidence, documentary or art-historical, is found either to
confirm or to disprove it.

Whoever designed the two frontispieces, their place in English architectural history needs to be defined. More sophisticated and cosmopoli-
tan than the 'artisan mannerism' of men like Peter Mills and Nicholas
Stone, they represent a baroque alternative to the Italian classicism of
Inigo Jones, of which there might well have been more examples but for
the Civil War. After half a century or so of architectural mannerism
largely Flemish in derivation, England in the reign of Charles I was ready
to assimilate a baroque architecture also largely Flemish in origin.[44] From
that natural development England was diverted by Inigo Jones, who
alone among northern European architects of his day renounced the baroque in favour of a return to the High Renaissance. By himself Jones
could hardly have stemmed the baroque tide, but the Civil War, the
decline of Antwerp, and the severing of English links with Catholic
Flanders in favour of Protestant Holland all tended to steer English architecture away from the exuberant baroque of the Canterbury Quadrangle
frontispieces and towards the discreet classicism of men such as Hugh
May and Roger Pratt. So the Canterbury Quadrangle is not only a
memorial to a great political prelate: it represents an architectural initiat-
ive that failed with the regime that he sustained.

✻   ✻   ✻

It is the interior of the Canterbury Quadrangle that gives it its special
place in English architectural history. But the garden front, so much
admired by Victorian taste, and so perfect, in its carefully calculated
asymmetry, as the background to an eighteenth-century landscape gar-

[43] PRO, SP 105/7–18.
[44] H. J. Louw, 'Anglo-Netherlandish Architectural Interchange *c.*1600–*c.*1660', *Architectural
History*, 24 (1981).

res at Hamstead Marshall

VIRTVS IN ACTIONE CONSISTIT.

Sr Balthazar Gerbier Baron Douly Fecit

46. Design for gateway at Hamstead Marshall, Berkshire, signed by Sir Baltha-zar Gerbier (Bodleian Library, Oxford, MS Gough Drawings a. 2, fos. 24–5)

den, is an important architectural entity in its own right (Fig. 74). It is essentially Gothic in style, with only some mannerist strapwork and the gateway from Francart's book to link it with the classical features within. Its architectural character was largely determined by the re-use of the east window from the Elizabethan library, which was moved out bodily to the line of the new east front (Fig. 47).[45] The other four oriel windows were made to the same traditional pattern, and their lower panels were carved

[45] See below, p. 57.

47. The oriel window at the east end of the Old Library

with strapwork cartouches 'answerable to the Bottome of the Greate Library window'.[46] Above, battlements and a string-course studded with grotesque heads maintained the picturesque character of a Gothic elevation. There was, however, a moment when circular windows were envisaged—indeed actually constructed—in the lower storey. Oval and circular windows were fashionable in the 1630s,[47] but here they would not have accorded well with the Tudor Gothic windows above, and it was doubtless for this reason that they were eventually suppressed, though internally their splays remain visible in the walls of the narrow passages beneath the Laudian Library. Whether they were completely to have replaced the two-light windows that now light these passages or to have alternated with them (Fig. 48) it is impossible to say. It may be added that the odd single-light window in the east wall (now lighting the space beneath the library staircase) appears to have been a later insertion, since in the building accounts of 1632–5 ironwork is provided for only four 'lower windows of the East Range' and glazing for only six lights in 'the lower chamber of the addition eastward to the Library', that is for three two-light windows, two in the south wall and one in the east, facing the garden.

[46] Building Accounts, p. 35.
[47] They were, for instance, used in the aisles of the church of St Giles-in-the-Fields, London, consecrated by Laud in 1631 (J. Parton, *Account of the Hospital and Parish of St Giles-in-the-Fields* (1822)). Other examples are the Stables at Wilton House, Wiltshire. (*c*.1628), the south front of Ashton Court, nr. Bristol (*c*.1628), and the river front of York House, Westminster, as illustrated in *The King's Arcadia*, ed. J. Harris, S. Orgel, and R. Strong (1973), fig. 390.

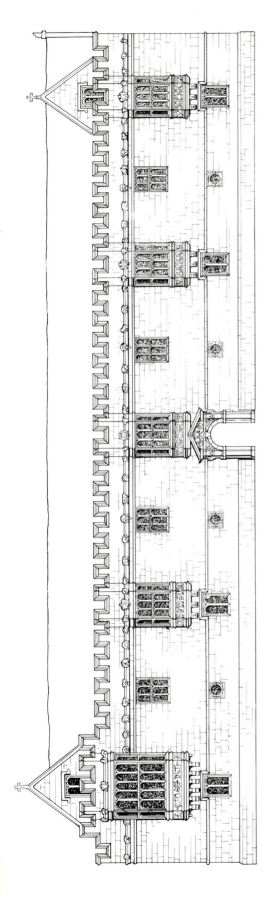
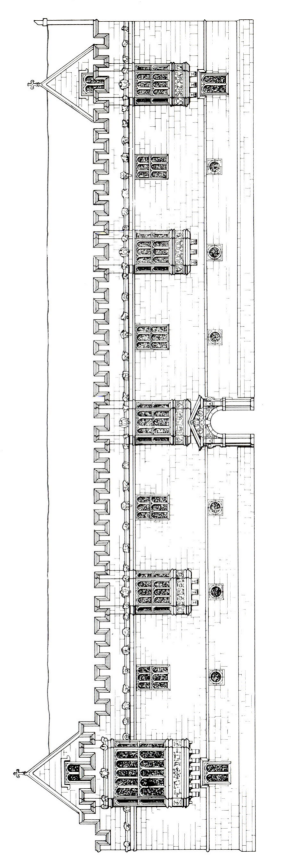

48. Conjectural drawings of the garden front of the Canterbury Quadrangle, with (*above*) round windows alternating with the existing two-light windows, and (*below*) replacing them. Round windows remain blocked up in the positions shown in the upper drawing. Compare with Fig. 74

3.

The Library

THE OLD LIBRARY

THE architectural character of the Canterbury Quadrangle was largely determined by the pre-existing library which formed its southern side. In 1631, when Laud began to build a matching wing to the north, the library was only thirty-four years old: Laud himself had been a junior fellow at the time it was built.

The decision to build the library was taken in November 1595, when the President and ten senior fellows (who then formed the governing body) agreed 'that a newe librarie be erected . . . for the enlarginge of roome and lodginges in the Colledge and for the better commoditie of the said Colledge and studentes in the same'.[1] The wording of the resolution suggests that the incentive to build the library was as much the need to provide more 'roome and lodginges' as to make better provision for books, and in correspondence with a potential benefactor the College stressed 'the wante of roome for the multytude of students' as well as the need for 'a Library for books'.[2] A new library might provide some additional living accommodation on its ground floor as well as releasing space in the old quadrangle at present occupied by books.[3]

The site chosen was to the east of the old quadrangle, and the College proposed at first to erect a building running north and south, with the southern end level with the boundary wall between St John's and Trinity College. The precise site envisaged cannot now be determined, nor is the preference for a north–south orientation explained, but in the event Trinity College refused to allow their neighbours to set up ladders and scaffolding on their ground, and the College decided to site the library on an east–west axis which would keep it well away from the party wall with Trinity.[4] The building whose foundations were laid in March 1596 was

---

[1] College Register, ii, 65. See also ibid. 86.
[2] Muniments, x. 12.
[3] This ambivalence of purpose may help to explain a curious feature of the building. The regular pattern of the floor beams is interrupted to provide slots for staircases corresponding to the two doorways to the chambers on the ground floor. Such staircases, coming up under the book-presses, would of course be incompatible with the use of the upper floor as a library, and they were never built, the spaces provided for them being filled up with cross-timbering.
[4] W. H. Stevenson and H. E. Salter, *Early History of St John's College* (1939), 294.

completely detached from the old quadrangle, and not on precisely the same alignment. Nevertheless it was so sited that a corresponding wing could be built to the north without obstructing the east end of the chapel, and the fact that the north side of the building was faced with ashlar while the south side was faced with thin courses of some inferior stone suggests that this eventuality was foreseen.

The new library appears to have been structurally complete by the end of 1598, though there was to be some further expenditure on 'finishinge' it in the course of the next year or two. The outlay amounted to at least £800, of which about half was contributed by the Merchant Taylors' Company and other benefactors. Only a summary account of the expenditure has been preserved,[5] and the names of the craftsmen are not recorded. Much stone and timber was economically obtained from the buildings of the former Carmelite friary on the western outskirts of the city, which belonged to the College. With the consent of the tenant, the 'great house, frame or buylding' standing on the site of the White Friars was demolished and its materials transported to the site of the new library.[6] The stone obtained in this way must have been used as rubble and in 1965–6 the recovery from the walls of the library of part of the capital of a two-light Romanesque window recalled the fact that the Carmelite friary had been established by King Edward II in the buildings of a royal residence much used by the Angevin kings of England in the twelfth century.[7]

Access to the library was by means of an external staircase at the west end. In 1633 this was described as 'the greate dubble staire case to the Library'[8] and in 1710 as 'a fine double stone staircase'.[9] It was replaced in 1796 by the present curved flight of stone stairs, built 'according to a Plan delivered in by Mr. Pears', that is the Oxford builder James Pears who had just erected the adjoining Holmes Building.[10]

On the ground floor there were four rooms, each designed for two occupants. Above there was a spacious library of eight bays terminating in an oriel window decorated with heraldic glass commemorating the generosity of the Merchant Taylors' Company and other benefactors.[11] In 1633–5 this building was extended twenty feet eastwards by Archbishop Laud as part of his scheme for a new quadrangle. The oriel window was, it seems, dismantled and re-erected in its present position.[12] On

---

[5] Muniments, lxxxi. 1; printed in W. H. Stevenson and H. E. Salter, 297–300.

[6] Muniments, lxi. 16.

[7] *History of the King's Works*, ed. H. M. Colvin, ii (1963), 986–7.

[8] Building Accounts, p. 36.

[9] Zacharias Conrad von Uffenbach, *Oxford in 1710*, ed. W. H. Quarrell (1928), 58.

[10] College Register, viii, 32.

[11] See below, pp. 111–12.

[12] No explicit statement to this effect can be found in the Building Accounts, but such payments as relate to this window are all consistent with the hypothesis that it was the old window re-used rather than a new one, notably the carving of the ornament on the other four bay-windows 'answer-

the north side of the extension a handsome classical portal gave access to the new Laudian Library, while on the south a second bay window (Fig. 49) was placed in line with it. This window contains painted glass with Laud's arms and the date 1636. There is reason to think that it was an afterthought, for it is not mentioned in the building accounts, which refer instead to the glazing of two two-light windows 'on the South side of the Addition of the Library Eastward towards Trinity College'.[13] The jamb of one of these two windows was seen built up in the wall immediately to the west of the bay window when the panelling was removed for repair in 1951.[14] So these two windows were evidently built *en suite* with the other library windows before a decision was made to substitute for them a larger window that would serve as a visual termination to the Laudian Library. Items of expenditure relating to this occur in a supplementary account rendered to Laud by President Baylie in 1636.[15] The mason John Jackson received £35. 17s. 6d. for works which included 'one Bay window in the olde Librarie', while a payment of £9. 6s. to the carpenter Edward Bromfield 'for timber and workemanship in raising the Bay window in the olde Librarie' would be for centering and consequential alterations to the roof.

As completed soon after 1598 the library conformed to what by the end of the sixteenth century was a well-established plan for academic and ecclesiastical libraries, with projecting furniture for chained books forming transverse bays containing wooden seats for the readers.[16] Each bay was lit by a two-light window and overhead there was a barrel-vaulted plaster ceiling rising from moulded wooden wall-plates. In earlier libraries the books were chained to sloping lecterns, but relatively few books could be accommodated in this manner, and in recent years some libraries had been adapted to a more efficient system in which blocks of shelves (known as 'presses') took the place of lecterns. Merton College had made the change in 1589–90, All Souls was in process of making it in 1596–7, and Sir Thomas Bodley was about to introduce it to Duke Humphrey's Library. New College, Corpus, Magdalen, and Christ Church would follow suit within the next few years.[17] St John's was, however, the first Oxford library to be designed specifically for the accommodation of books in presses, with desks rather than lecterns on which to read them.

---

able to the Bottome of the Greate Library window' (p. 35). It was already back in place by June 1634, when Anthony Gore was paid 15s. 'for clensinge the carvinge of the Greate East Window of the Librarye' (p. 7).

[13] Building Accounts, p. 50.

[14] A photograph is preserved in the College archives (lxxxii. 221).

[15] PRO SP 16/319, fo. 38 (76).

[16] See J. W. Clark, *The Care of Books* (Cambridge 1901) and B. H. Streeter, *The Chained Library* (1931).

[17] J. N. L. Myres, 'Oxford Libraries in the Seventeenth and Eighteenth Centuries', in *The English Library before 1700*, ed. F. Wormald and C. E. Wright (1958) and N. R. Ker, 'Oxford College Libraries in the Sixteenth Century', *Bodleian Library Record*, 6 (1959).

49. The bay window built in 1636 on the south side of the
Old Library

50. One of the presses in the Old Library (*Country Life*)

Although at first sight the interior of the library presents a vista of presses that looks entirely homogeneous (Fig. 51), it soon becomes evident on closer examination that the apparent uniformity conceals a sequence of alterations and adaptations. Some presses are of later date than others, many have had their shelving altered, and all have been heightened at some time. Moreover there is an obvious contrast between the rough craftsmanship of the archaic-looking benches and the much more sophisticated joiner's work of the intervening presses, each crowned with a moulded and modillioned pediment decorated with urns (Fig. 50). Several of the benches themselves prove on examination to have mortices cut in their ends that do not fit the existing moulded rails. Even the 'bearers' or sill-beams that form the foundation for both presses and benches appear to have been re-used, for the presses rise from mortice-holes that are generally several inches longer than is necessary, while some of the bench-ends do not fit their allotted spaces with proper precision.

These discrepancies are capable of various interpretations: they may represent defective workmanship, second thoughts, subsequent alteration, or the re-use of older materials. Canon Streeter, who drew attention to some of them in his book *The Chained Library* (1931), considered

51. The interior of the Old Library, looking east (*Jim Chambers*)

that the moulded and pedimented tops to the presses were later in date than the presses themselves. If this was so, lower and simpler presses might have been contemporary with the primitive benches. But although the cornices and pediments were at some time raised eighteen inches by the insertion of a piece of timber of that size, there are in the ends of both presses and cornices pairs of corresponding dowel-holes which prove that the cornices were original features of the unheightened presses. If (as seems probable) the majority of the presses date from *c*.1598–9, then the benches may pre-date the building of the library. One possibility is that they were transferred from the old library in the Front Quadrangle. That library had been enlarged and partly refitted as recently as 1582–4,[18] and it would be an obvious economy to re-use as much as possible of its furniture. Of course the old library must have been substantially smaller than the new one. But of the sixteen benches in the present library, only seven are of precisely the same size and pattern. All the others differ in some respect. It will be shown later that four of them are certainly of later date, and if a nucleus of earlier benches was available others could doubtless have been made to match in *c*.1598–9. Indeed the fitting up of the new library was evidently to some extent a continuing process, for in 1602–3 there was considerable expenditure on 'new deskes', chains, and ironwork, and a joiner was paid £3. 0*s*. 8*d*. 'for x under desks in the Library'.[19] However the evidence is interpreted, the possibility remains that a number of the benches formed part of some other library before they were set up in the present one. But if the benches were re-used, why not the presses also? The answer is that the former library in the Front Quadrangle was constructed on the lectern system: this, as N. R. Ker pointed out, is apparent from the chain-marks on the bindings of books acquired before 1596. These marks are in the positions appropriate for lecterns, not for presses.[20] So the benches and the sill-beams would be re-usable, but not the obsolete lecterns, though there may be a trace of them in the long mortice-holes in the beams.

The new library appears therefore to have consisted of up-to-date presses alternating with benches of old-fashioned workmanship. The presses were eighteen inches lower than they are at present, and they were fitted with the paraphernalia of rods, chains, and locks that can still be seen in the library at Corpus Christi College. At St John's all that remains of this is holes for some of the rods beneath the desks, the neatly repaired scars of the locks in the ends of the presses, a score of loose chains, and

[18] W. H. Stevenson and H. E. Salter, 244, 254. See also pp. 106–7.
[19] College Archives, *Computus Annuus* 1602, fos. 112ᵛ–14; 1603, fo. 138.
[20] Ker, op. cit., 511.

INCHES 12 6 0   1   2   3   4   5   6 FEET

52. The westernmost bay on the north side of the Old Library, showing the benches, the heightened presses, and the panelling. Note the gap between the two lengths of sill-beam beneath the end of the press

the marks of many more on the covers of those books that have not been rebound in modern times.

The number of both presses and benches was, however, smaller than it is today. This is most apparent at the west end of the library, where panelling with a modillion cornice defines what was evidently a vestibule inside the entrance (Fig. 52). Presses S and Ω stand against the panelling and are clearly of later date. This is confirmed by minor differences in their construction, by the slightly different profile of their urns, and by the way the lateral panelling on both sides is cut off at the original height of the half-presses Q and Φ—a tell-tale detail now only visible on close inspection behind the ends of the later half-presses R and Ψ. The existing benches in this end bay are also obviously of later construction, as are the sill-beams on which they stand. Evidence from other libraries suggests that this vestibule would have contained boxes and cupboards for the safe-keeping of small books and manuscripts and that the catalogue would have been displayed there.[21] It is possible, as Streeter thought, that there was a screen separating the vestibule from the main body of the library, but if so no structural evidence of it remains.

At the east end there is some evidence of a similar arrangement before the extension of the library in 1633–5. Presses D/E and W/X are of later construction, while B/C and U/V each consists of two half-presses placed back to back. Before 1633 it is likely that there was one half-press as in Figure 53a. When Laud's work was nearly complete he directed that 'the Additions which I have made at the east end of the Lybrary shall goe to the Enlargement thereof with such deskes for chained Bookes as are allready in other parts of the Lybrary'.[22] The building accounts duly record payments of £8. 10s. 0d. to David Woodfield, joiner, for making '2 new deskes answerable to the ould' and '2 new seates', and of £3. 10s. 10d. to Thomas Addams, smith, for locks, hasps, bars, and hinges for the new desks.[23] From the details given of the ironwork, it appears that what Woodfield made was two complete new presses, one on either side of the library, together with two new back-to-back benches.[24] These are probably presses D/E and W/X which, together with the adjoining benches, show signs of later construction.[25] At the same time the two half-presses C and V would seem to have been resited further east, ultimately to form, with B and U, a second pair of complete presses. The joiner was also paid 12s. 'for altering the ould wainscott, taking it downe and setting it up againe'. This was probably the panelling at the east end of the library, some of which (despite its uniform appearance) may therefore be work of the 1590s reset in 1633–5. It is similar to the panelling at the west end, but the moulded cornice differs slightly in profile.

[21] Streeter, op. cit. 196. In Hereford Cathedral Library the upper end was wainscotted and contained 'a fayre waynescot desk thereon to keepe a catalogue of the bookes in the Librarie with the names of the donors & a table to leane or write on by them that should come to looke on that booke or catalogue' (*Journal of the National Library of Wales*, 6 (1949–50), 363). The St John's accounts show that in 1604 a book was purchased 'to wright in the Catalog of the Library books' (*Computus Annuus* 1604, fo. 164). Evidence that manuscripts were kept in this part of the library is afforded by the title formerly painted over the conjoined half-presses Q and R, which read 'VARII & MS^{ti}' (i.e. MANUSCRIPTI) (see below p. 114). The provision of 'boxes for small books' is mentioned in the College Register in 1602 (ii, 217).

[22] College Register, iii, 141.

[23] Building Accounts, p. 65.

[24] Addams supplied four locks and hasps, four long and eight short bars and eight pairs of hinges. A long bar ran the length of each half-press just below desk level, where the holes for its passage can still be seen. Above there would have been two short bars at first-shelf level, where their ends met in a central metal fastening whose outline can still be seen on many of the presses. Streeter was evidently right in concluding that there were no bars at second-shelf level except possibly at the west end of the library.

[25] The presses were made with three instead of two shelves, the four pairs of hinges differ slightly in design from the others, and the bench-ends are thinner and more regularly made than the older ones. The pediments and urns have a different profile which they share, however, with those on presses B/C and U/V.

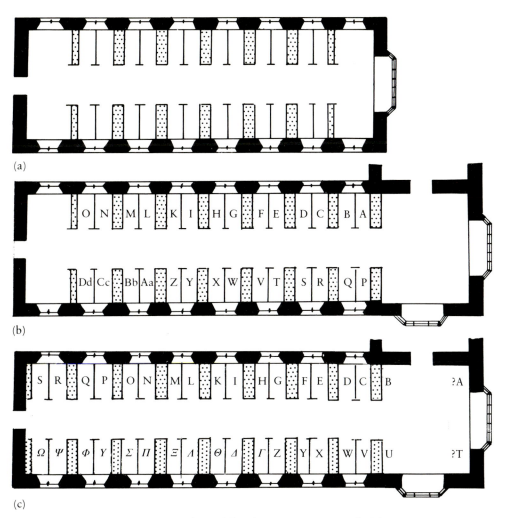

53. Plans of the presses in the Old Library. (a) as probably arranged before 1633; (b) as arranged and lettered before 1746; and (c) as lettered since 1746

These conclusions, based on structural evidence and partly confirmed by the accounts, are reinforced by the system of shelf-marks shown in Figure 53b. These shelf-marks were painted on the presses, and are still faintly visible beneath the eighteenth-century paint. It will be seen that the sequence of letters included the two new presses probably made in 1633–5, but not the four half-presses now occupying the vestibule at the west end, which must presumably have been made at a later date. This system of lettering is distinguished from that now in use (and instituted probably in 1746) by the double letters Aa–Dd and the absence of Greek letters. As the same system is reflected in the earliest surviving catalogue of the Old Library, started apparently in 1687–8, it follows that the four half-presses at the west end were probably added after that date. This is

54. A pediment bent back at right angles over one of the half-presses at the west end of the Old Library (*Jim Chambers*)

consistent with an architectural detail that distinguishes the two half-presses standing against the west wall of the library (Fig. 54). Their pediments are bent back at right angles in a manner paralleled both in late Antiquity (e.g. the Arch of Septimius Severus at Lepcis Magna in North Africa) and in Piedmontese baroque of *c*.1700 (Sta. Maria del Popolo, Cherasco).[26] Even if at St John's the form was evolved empirically to avoid the awkwardness of a half-pediment, it is unlikely that such a baroque expedient would have commended itself at an earlier date.

As originally constructed all the Elizabethan presses had only two shelves above the desk. Presses D/E and W/X (the ones believed to have been made in 1633–5) were, however, of a modified type with three shelves, and at some subsequent date the older presses were all adapted by lowering the existing shelves and inserting a third one.[27] Finally every press

[26] Both illustrated by M. Lyttelton, *Baroque Architecture in Classical Antiquity* (1974), pl. 2 and fig. 50.

[27] Streeter's theory that the desks were originally seven inches higher and were lowered at the same time as the shelves is difficult to sustain, as there is no indication whatever on the ends of the presses that the desks were ever fixed at a different height. However (like so much of the library woodwork), many of the desk-flaps do, as Streeter pointed out, show signs of having been re-used, for the outlines of quite different supports can be discerned on their undersides.

was heightened by eighteen inches, thus providing space for cupboards immediately beneath the reset cornice. These cupboards were for the safe keeping of smaller books which could not conveniently be chained. There were two of them on each side and the marks of their locks and hinges are still clearly visible. Traces of locks can be seen in comparable positions in the Arts End of the Bodleian Library, and similar cupboards actually survive in the libraries of Lincoln and The Queen's Colleges.[28]

The date when the additional shelves were inserted is uncertain,[29] but the cupboards were constructed in 1736, in response to a resolution that 'all the books in the College be chain'd, excepting the small ones, which are not fit for chains, and may be enclosed more conveniently in cells contrived for that purpose'.[30] The smith's bill for that year charges for 136 pairs of hinges and sixty-eight locks—precisely the number required for the sixty-eight 'cells' or cupboards. It therefore follows that the heightening of the shelves by eighteen inches must have taken place at the same time, and this was probably part of the work for which the carpenter Jeremiah Franklin was paid £122. 13s. $11\frac{1}{4}d.$ that year.[31]

As in other Oxford libraries the system of chained books remained in use at St John's until well into the eighteeth century. The date when it was finally abandoned was not formally recorded, but when the College received a major accession of over a thousand books in 1745 no attempt appears to have been made to chain them. These books were the legacy of Nathaniel Crynes, one of the Esquire Bedells, and in his will he originally left £40 'to be expended & paid out in making so many Presses with lattices lock and keys in St. John's College Library after the manner of All Souls Library as will contain the octavos and other smaller Books'.[32] But probably realizing that it would be difficult to find any space for wall-cases on the All Souls model, Crynes subsequently cancelled this clause, leaving his books to be housed as the College thought fit. None of Crynes's books shows signs of having been chained, and although there was expenditure in 1746 which shows that some books were still chained,[33] it is likely that the practice of chaining fell into disuse thereafter

---

[28] Both illustrated by Streeter, op. cit. 233, 251.

[29] The joiner who made press W/X scribed the outer end for only two shelves, as elsewhere in the library, but then made it with three. So it looks as if W/X was the first press made to the new design and the innovation can probably be dated to 1633–5. Exactly when the other presses were altered to match has not been ascertained, but it must have been before they were heightened in 1736.

[30] College Register, vii, 61.

[31] Smith's bill in College Archives, Acc. V.B.; *Computus Annuus* 1735–6, p. 48. The doors of the cupboards may have incorporated a lattice of wire, for J. Newman was paid £12. 7s. 6d. 'for wire-work done in the Library' (ibid. 45).

[32] College Register, vii, 169–71.

[33] The smith's bill for 1746–7 included, under the Library heading, 'two new cups for the Bars', eighty 'S hooks to the Chains', and 'three men one day & two men another day fixing 'em to the Chains' (Acc. V.B).

and that all the chains had been removed before the end of the century.[34]

A memorandum in the Library Benefactors' Book indicates that the Crynes bequest led to a review of the contents of the library and to a general repair and redecoration of the building itself.[35] This included taking down and rebuilding 'the great bow window at the south-east corner of the library', much reglazing of the windows, restoring and repainting the woodwork, repairing the catalogue frames on the ends of the presses, and writing new titles beneath the cornices.[36] These are evidently the existing titles, beneath which an earlier set of titles, dating presumably from the seventeenth century, can be discerned (see below, p. 114). Both emphasize the predominantly religious and scholastic character of the library, though the provision made by the Founder for the study of Civil Law and Medicine is reflected in presses devoted to those subjects, while Natural History, Mathematics, Greek and Latin Classics, History and Chronology, Archaeology and Geography, were all represented by 1746.

The interior of the Old Library underwent no further change until the nineteenth century. The date when the cupboard doors were removed does not appear to have been recorded, but the unpainted shelves standing against the ends of the presses in the central aisle must be the sixteen 'Bookcases' for which one Prattley was paid £29. 8s. in 1861.[37] Their erection would have entailed the removal of the moulded wooded catalogue frames which (as in other Oxford libraries) contained lists of the books in each press. Valuable though the additional shelf-space was (and still is), these cases detract considerably from the visual appearance of the Old Library.

A much more drastic alteration was the removal in 1884–5 of the plaster ceiling of the Old Library. This was preparatory to the repair of the timber roof, whose unsatisfactory construction had long been a source of trouble. The decision to remove the barrel-vaulted plaster ceiling was taken by the Estates Committee on 21 October 1884, and on 28

[34] The removal of chains in the Bodleian Library began in 1757, at Brasenose the books were unchained in 1780, at Merton in 1792 (J. W. Clark, *The Care of Books* (Cambridge, 1901), 266).

[35] *Registrum Benefactorum Bibliothecae*, col. 449: 'Cum annis proxime elapsis permagna Librorum Copia Musaeo nostro accesserit, visum est Bibliothecario Bibliothecae penitus reformandae graviter Operam dare, Libros ex rudi indigesto Cumulo pro diversa singulorum Materia, quatenus licuit, in certas Classes distribuere, et insuper, ne in tanta Multitudine quisquam tum, cum maxime quaeratur, delitesceret, eorum Indicem sive Repertorium triplex contexere, viz. Tacticum, Alphabeticum, Hylicum. Collegiales interea, ut haec Aedes Musarum, Re literaria tam locuples, Ornatu pariter ac Usu emineret, Aedificium ipsum extrinsecus et intrinsecus et reparandum et decorandum statuerunt.'

[36] As recorded in the respective mason's, carpenter's, glazier's, and painter's bills (Acc. V.B). The number of letters accounted for in the painter's bill considerably exceeds the number required for the titles in the Old Library and must include some lettering in the Laudian Library.

[37] Library Accounts 1812–61 (Admin. VII. C.1).

November the Committee directed the Bursar 'to employ Mr. Moore to survey the library roof and to report on the cost and advisability of making a roof over the rafters as before, or restoring the old open roof as seen at the east end' *(sic)*.[38] Mr Moore was H. W. Moore of Wilkinson and Moore, the architects employed as supervisory surveyors of the College's North Oxford Estate. His report has not survived, but a clue as to its contents is provided by a report in the *Oxford Chronicle* for 17 October 1885 that 'a new panelled oak ceiling has been placed in the Library [at St John's College] from the design of Messrs. Wilkinson and Moore, architects'. No such ceiling was in fact executed, and in 1887–8 the problem of the library roof was dealt with by J. J. Stevenson as part of the general repair of the Canterbury Quadrangle (see pp. 99–100). Stevenson prevented further movement of the roof by the insertion of attractively designed iron tie-rods, and made good the ceiling by the simple expedient of plastering between the rafters instead of restoring the Elizabethen barrel-vault. The result is picturesque and not unattractive, but the irregularity of the rafters makes it apparent that their exposure was not intended by the original builders of the library.

During the first half of the twentieth century the Old Library remained essentially as it had been left in 1888. An attack of death-watch beetle was dealt with by Messrs Richardson and Starling of Winchester in 1950; the panelling at the east end was repaired in 1951; the painted shelf-marks were renewed in 1953; and concealed fluorescent lighting was installed on the tops of the presses in 1960. A major enlargement of the library was, however, undertaken in 1970. This had two objectives: substantially to increase the accommodation for both books and readers, and to provide a central entrance foyer to control the ingress and egress of readers and the issue and return of books. These aims reflected the recent increase in the graduate and undergraduate population of the College, and the problem of security at a time when thefts of books from libraries were widespread. They were achieved by the conversion of the four rooms beneath the Old Library into a new Lower Library, the creation of a foyer on the ground floor, with an entrance from the east cloister (where a new doorway had already been made in 1965), and the insertion of a new internal staircase for regular use instead of the external one at the west end of the building. These works, completed in 1976, were designed by Mr Walter Price of the Oxford Architects Partnership in collaboration with the present writer, then Librarian. They were carried out

---

[38] Estates Committee Minutes, 21 Oct. and 28 Nov. 1884. Presumably a section of the ceiling had already been removed at the east end for exploratory purposes. There had, of course, never been an 'open roof'.

in two stages, the first by Messrs Hinkins and Frewen, the second by the staff of the College's own Estates Yard. On the ground floor the timber-framed partitions between the rooms were necessarily removed, but the existing panelling was retained and reproduced where necessary. Upstairs the new staircase beneath the east window was designed in such a way as not to interfere with the view down the library from the west end. By these means the seating capacity of the library was increased by thirty-six places, and the book capacity by some 20,000 volumes.

THE LAUDIAN LIBRARY

The eastern side of the Canterbury Quadrangle is occupied by what is now called the Laudian Library, but was for long known simply as the Inner Library. In the building accounts of 1633–5 it is generally referred to as 'the Gallery'.[39] It extends the whole length of the eastern cloister and is lighted by windows facing the quadrangle on one side and the garden on the other. At ground floor level the vaulted passageway to the garden passes beneath it, and on either side are the narrow storage spaces known as the Otranto Passages.

The foundation stone of the 'Library addition' was laid on 11 November 1633, when 2s. 6d. was given to the masons Richard Piddington and William Badger who built it.[40] It was structurally complete by the summer of 1635, when great efforts were made to get it finished in time for Laud's visit on 3 September. The plasterers were paid an extra 20s. to complete their work 'before his Grace's comming to Oxford', and a similar sum was spent on washing down 'to gett of[f] the lime'.[41] A year later it provided the setting for Laud's great entertainment of the King and Queen.[42]

No plan or drawing survives of the Laudian Library as it existed in the seventeenth and eighteenth centuries, but it is clear that the decorative exuberance of the quadrangle did not extend to the interior. The only architectural ornament was the great stone doorway at the south end, surmounted by Laud's arms and mitre (Fig. 55). It is known that the ceiling was 'of arched plaster, and perfectly plain'.[43] Above it was a 'cant roof' framed in such a way as to accommodate the plasterwork. This meant that there could be no tie-beams, but the roof was better constructed than the one on the Old Library. It consisted of twelve

[39] Building Accounts, pp. 33, 37, 46, etc.
[40] Ibid. 82.
[41] Ibid. 38, 83.
[42] See above, p. 13.
[43] *Anastatic Drawing Society*, vol. for 1857, p. 6.

55. The door-cases framing the entrance to the Laudian Library, showing the original wooden doors and (on the north side) the arms of Archbishop Laud (*Jim Chambers*)

pairs of principal rafters with arch-braces and collars and these were 'secured from thrusting out' by massive bolts made of 'extraordinary iron'.[44]

In October 1635, Laud indicated the use to which he intended the new library to be put. It was to be

for an Inner Library in which may be kept the Manuscripts, and all smaller Bookes, which might otherwise be in danger of looseing. Or any other Rarity which may in after times be given to that Colledge. As allsoe all Mathematicall Bookes and Instruments which myselfe . . . or any other shall give unto that Colledge.[45]

For these purposes presses like those in the Old Library would not be suitable, and instead Laud provided cases with lockable doors. There were seven of them, and they were designed to stand flat against the walls between the windows. A German visitor in 1710 described them as 'two rows of locked bookcases with latticed doors'.[46] Owing to the spacing of the windows, the arrangement of the cases cannot have been completely symmetrical. On the west side there was room for two or at the most three in the centre, while up to six could have been placed against the east wall (cf. Fig. 78). The most striking feature of the presses was their pierced metal grilles, decorated with their donor's arms, crest (a lark) and mitre (Fig. 56). As pieces of movable furniture rather than fixtures the Laudian bookcases do not have the innovatory importance of the wall-shelving introduced into the Bodleian Library in 1610–12. Nevertheless the Laudian Library was the first college library in either Oxford or Cambridge to be arranged on the new principle. Its function as a 'Mathematical Library' was emphasized by the Greek inscription Ὁ ΘΕΟΣ μάλιστα παντων γεωμετρει ('God is the greatest geometer of all') with a scale and compasses, over the entrance from the Old Library (Fig. 55).

The furnishing of the Laudian Library was a gradual process which extended over several years. It is not well documented, and there is no explicit reference to the Laudian bookcases. In 1637/8 President Baylie, on Laud's behalf, paid £50 to 'Mr. Richarson [*a joiner*] for his workemanshipp in frameing and setting up the wainscott in the new Library according unto a Draft presented unto his Grace'.[47] The wainscot is mentioned by the Frenchman Samuel Sorbière in 1664,[48] but nothing is known of its design. Another payment by Baylie for the carriage of fir boards from London 'according to direction received from Mr. Adam

---

[44] Building Accounts, p. 47. In Aug. 1635 the carpenter Edward Bromfield went up to London 'to know my Lord of London's [*i.e. Juxon's*] pleasure about the cant roofe' (ibid. 83).

[45] College Register, iii, 141.

[46] von Uffenbach, op. cit. 58.

[47] PRO, SP 16/39, fo. 106.

[48] S. Sorbière, *A Voyage to England* (1709), 42: 'a large wainscotted gallery'.

56. One of the Laudian cases

Browne' is evidence of Browne's continued involvement in Laud's works at St John's. In May 1636 Laud himself paid Browne 12*s*. 'for a pedestall sent to St. Jo: Coll.', and in January 1638/9 £9. 6*s*. 6*d*. for work which included 'the case of the Anotomy'.[49] This recalls another feature of the Laudian Library, the two articulated skeletons or 'anatomies' which were presented by Dr John Speed (1595–1640), son of the cartographer and a fellow of the College. Such skeletons, holding moralizing scrolls, were a feature of the famous anatomical theatre at Leiden, and were used for medical demonstrations.[50] A drawing of the St John's 'anatomies', made by Speed himself, shows them standing on either side of a doorway in just such cases as the one Browne would have made for Laud (Fig. 57). As Anthony Wood, writing later in the century, describes them as 'standing at the north end of the mathematic library of the college',[51] it follows that there was a doorway from the Laudian Library into the room beyond. This doorway was blocked up later, but traces of it were found when the room was altered in 1937.[52]

Laud continued to present books, manuscripts, and mathematical

[49] PRO, E101/547/5 (Laud's household accounts for 1635–51), fo. 94.

[50] W. Heckscher, *Rembrandt's Anatomy of Dr Nicholas Tulp* (New York, 1958).

[51] A. Wood, *Athenae Oxonienses*, ed. P. Bliss (1813–20), ii, 660.

[52] Bursary file 220, fo. 73.

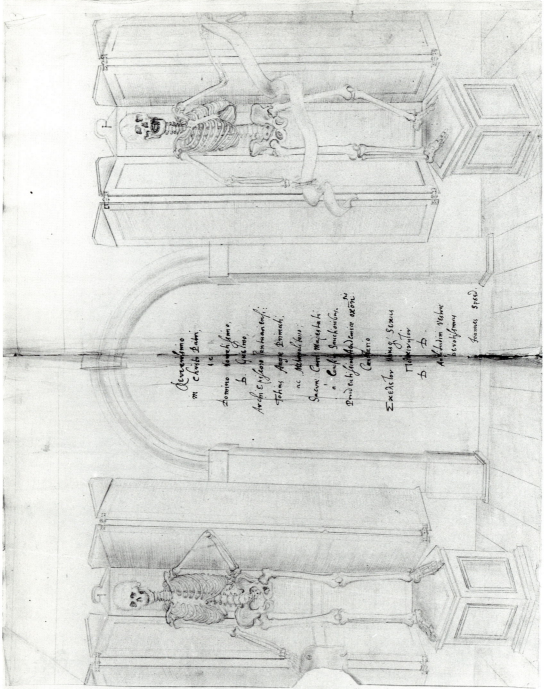

57. The two skeletons that originally stood on either side of the doorway (now blocked) at the north end of the Laudian Library, from a drawing by their donor, John Speed (St John's College Library, MS 22)

instruments to the library up to and indeed after the time of his imprisonment. Sending an astrolabe in May 1638, he expressed pleasure at hearing 'that my Mathematicke Library is in such forwardnes', and hoped that 'you will see some shutt[er]s made before the shelves to keepe both books and instruments in better safety'.[53] In June 1639 he sent six maps 'made up after the newest and best fashion for use', 'to be placed in my Mathematick Library', together with 'nine manuscripts, some Arabick, some Greeke, for the better furnishing of that Library; they being all mathematicall'.[54] And in September 1641, writing from the Tower about the regulations for the use of the library, he says that he had 'made deskes and boxes, with lockes and keyes, thorough all the Library, to secure [the manuscripts] from losse'.[55] These pieces of furniture are described in a contemporary document as 'certayne Deskes or Archives all under severall lockes and keyes'.[56] As the latticed cupboards in the Bodleian Library are referred to in one of Sir Thomas Bodley's letters as 'grated desks'[57] and have subsequently been known as *Archiva*, it is possible that by 'desks and boxes' Laud meant the existing latticed cases. It would certainly be surprising if they were not in place in the library by 1641. A list of them, with their distinguishing letters, is prefaced to a catalogue of books and manuscripts in the Laudian Library drawn up in about 1670;[58] it is as follows:

(1) A. Mathematical Instruments
(2) B. Books elegantly bound
(3) C. Manuscripts
(4) D. Manuscripts
(5) E. Walton's Polyglot Bible (*added later*)
(6) F.
(7) G. Mathematical Books

In the course of time these seven cases were supplemented by other cases or shelves,[59] but the Laudian Library remained substantially unaltered until 1838–9, when it was completely transformed. The plaster ceiling was taken down to expose the structural timbers, which were modified to form an open roof, decked out with plaster angels, shields, and mitres, the wainscot was stripped from the walls, and the leaded

[53] College Register, iii, 208.
[54] College Register, iii, 239.
[55] College Register, iii, 308.
[56] College Register, iii, 309.
[57] *Letters of Sir Thomas Bodley to Thomas James*, ed. G. W. Wheeler (1926), 22.
[58] College Archives, Fin. V.A.9.
[59] The painter's account for 1747 includes a charge for 'painting the edges of the new shelves' in the Inner Library and the description of the library in the Anastatic Drawing Society's volume for 1857, after describing the Laudian cases, mentions 'two or three others made of deal, with panels of open work like the plainer panels of the original book-cases, but with no panels containing the more elaborate devices found on . . . the older or oaken book-cases'.

casements were replaced by sash windows. All the Laudian cases, with their beautiful and unusual grilles, were sold.[60] In their place open book-shelves were constructed at right angles to the walls, solid, useful, and conscientiously Gothic. What had been a remarkable survival from the reign of Charles I was transformed into a Victorian working library. The whole operation was carried out by the Oxford builder John Hudson under the direction of H. J. Underwood (1804–52), an architect who had recently established himself in Oxford, where he had already remodelled part of Exeter College and designed two churches, one in Summertown, the other for J. H. Newman at Littlemore.[61] He was a competent Gothicist who enjoyed the approval of the Oxford Architectural Society, and his redesigning of the Laudian Library was by no means ill done (Fig. 58). The total destruction, without record, of the authentic Laudian interior, and the dispersal of the original furniture was, however, an act of vandal-ism on the part of the President and fellows which demonstrated a total lack of the respect due to the memory of a great benefactor, as well as an undiscriminating contempt for anything that was not Gothic. But in the 1830s there was little disposition to cherish the memory of Archbishop Laud at St John's. In the recent past there had been a strong evangelical element among its fellows.[62] The President, Philip Wynter, was as Vice-Chancellor to suspend the High Church Dr Pusey for heresy and (accord-ing to College tradition) to allow the College's collection of pre-Reforma-tion vestments (then kept in the Lodgings) to be used by his children for the performance of charades. The destruction of Laud's library was fol-lowed by a similar remodelling of the chapel, in the course of which everything Caroline or Georgian was replaced by the banal Gothic of Edward Blore and the monument to Laud's nephew-in-law President Baylie was barbarously dismembered. It is fortunate that the College's rumoured intention to treat the Old Library in similar fashion was not fulfilled.[63]

Nevertheless, it must be admitted that in its new guise the Laudian

[60] They were sold for £4 each (*Computus Annuus* 1841, p. 18 and Library Accounts 1841). Two were bought by President Wynter and have remained in the President's Lodgings ever since. Four were acquired by fellows, one by G. T. Clare, who took it with him to his Rectory at Bainton in Yorkshire, and one each by J. A. Hessey, L. A. Sharpe, and A. B. C. Starkey. In 1871 Clare's was bought by the owner of the nearby Neswick Hall, whence it was recovered by purchase in 1946. Hessey's was given by his widow to Lambeth Palace Library some time after his death in 1892, but the provenance of a second case now at Lambeth is not known. Nor is the source known of a second case

purchased by the College in 1959. Some further 'old Library Cases' had, however, been sold by the College in 1841 to the Oxford furniture dealer Mallam. All the surviving cases have been altered to a greater or lesser extent and two of the three now in the President's Lodgings are little more than nineteenth-century cupboards which incorporate grilles from Laudian cases.

[61] Hudson's account, with Underwood's signa-ture, is in the College Muniments, lxxxi. 19.

[62] J. S. Reynolds, *The Evangelicals at Oxford 1735–1871* (Appleford, 1975), 69, 81, 155.

[63] *The Stranger's Guide and Historical and Biographical Hand-book to Oxford* (n.d.), 137.

58. The interior of the Laudian Library, looking north (*Jim Chambers*)

Library was to serve the College well for over a century. By 1913 the Gothic bookshelves, originally about fifteen in number, had been increased to twenty, and housed a working library of some 10,000 volumes.[64] Gone were the miscellaneous curiosities that had been noted by Celia Fiennes in 1694 and ridiculed by Nicholas Amhurst in 1726.[65] The two skeletons had long been removed to a room called the Museum (apparently the one on the ground floor at the north end of the east cloister).[66] There they had joined a large collection of natural specimens bequeathed by the scientific antiquary John Pointer in 1754.[67] In 1829 the Museum was taken over as an undergraduate's room and its contents were relegated to the northern Otranto Passage, whence, after nearly a century of neglect, what was left of them was transferred in 1925 to the newly established Lewis Evans Collection (now the Museum of the History of Science) in Broad Street.[68]

Throughout the eighteenth and nineteenth centuries the use of both Old and Laudian Libraries was reserved exclusively for fellows. In 1868 an Undergraduate Library was established for the use of men reading for Honours and in 1887 this was transferred from the Front Quadrangle to what is now Room C 4,1 on the north side of the Canterbury Quadrangle. A Gothic doorway was made in the north wall of the cloister to give access to it.[69] It was not until 1933 that the Laudian Library, after some rearrangement, was opened to junior members of the College.[70] Since then two of the Laudian bookcases sold in 1841 have been recovered by purchase, one in 1946, and the other in 1959.[71] These two cases now stand at the ends of the Lower and Laudian Libraries, respectively, and are used to house the College's manuscripts. In 1985 the surviving metal grilles from a third case, found in 1951 in a cellar beneath the Holmes Building, were made up into two smaller cases to contain a collection of books relating to A. E. Housman, partly purchased by the College after his death in 1936, and partly presented by Mr John Sparrow in 1984. Thus the twentieth century, without renouncing the utility of the Laudian Library in its Victorian form, has done something to atone for the vandalism which accompanied its transformation in 1838–9.

[64] College Register, x, 391, 482. The Gothic cresting was removed from all but three of the bookcases in 1941 (Library Committee Minutes, 5 Nov. 1941). Fluorescent lighting was installed on top of them in 1964.

[65] *The Journeys of Celia Fiennes*, ed. C. Morris (1949), 35; N. Amhurst, *Terrae Filius* (1726) ii, 21.

[66] Wood, op. cit. ii, 660.

[67] For the *Museum Pointerianum* see R. T. Gunther, *Early Science in Oxford*, iii (1925), 336–41.

[68] College Register, viii, 401, 3 July 1829; Col-

lege Register, x, 622, 629; Gunther, *Early Science in Oxford*, xv (1967), 377. The two skeletons had already been given to George Rolleston, the first Linacre Professor of Anatomy, soon after 1860, to form part of his celebrated collection of skeletal remains, and, as part of that collection, are now in the University Museum. (Ref. nos. 14886–7)ı

[69] College Register, x, 66, 251, 273.

[70] College Register, xi, 55; Library Committee Minutes, 7 Mar. 1934.

[71] For the history of these cases, see above, n. 60.

4.

The President's Lodgings

A PART of the College that gained considerably from the building of the Canterbury Quadrangle was the President's Lodgings, which occupied the northern part of the eastern range of the Front Quadrangle. To allow the new quadrangle to be built the President had to give up part of his garden, and in 1630 it was Laud's intention 'to give the President a lower and an upper chamber joyning to his lodgings in lewe of part of his garden taken awaye'.[1] From an inventory drawn up in 1615 it appears that the President's Lodgings then consisted of a hall, kitchen, buttery, great chamber, parlour, and several other chambers, including some sort of gallery.[2] But the Lodgings were (as Laud was well aware) 'much too small',[3] and the building of the new quadrangle afforded an opportunity to enlarge them. On its completion in 1635, Laud informed the College that he wished 'to assigne and decree to the President's Lodgings' the greater part of the gallery over the western cloister, and 'that entyre part of the building which joynes to his Lodginge from the foundacion to the roofe, conteyning upon the ground a Buttery with Cellarage underneath it, a Kitchen, two Larders, two Chambers over them, and the Cocklofts, but noe more.'[4] In the decree by which the College gave effect to Laud's intention, this was rendered as 'on the north side, part of the building which adjoins the President's Lodging extending 39 feet eastwards, from the ground to the roof'.[5] Externally nothing showed where the President's Lodgings ended and the commoners' sets began, and internally there were no stone walls, only timber partitions. The dimension of thirty-nine feet seems to have been arbitrarily determined (perhaps by dividing by three the length of the north wall between the cloisters, which was just over 117 feet). It certainly did not correspond at all precisely to the dimensions of the presidential accommodation on the north side of the Canterbury Quadrangle as it existed in the seventeenth century, for the principal room extended well over forty feet eastwards from the old lodgings, and there was a second one beyond that.

The fitting up of the new part of the Lodgings and some of the consequential alterations to the old part can be followed in the building

[1] PRO, SP 6/172, fo. 68 ('Mye Intentions for Charitye').

[2] Muniments, xc. 10.

[3] College Register, iii, 144 (in Latin).

[4] College Register, iii, 142.

[5] College Register, iii, 144 (in Latin).

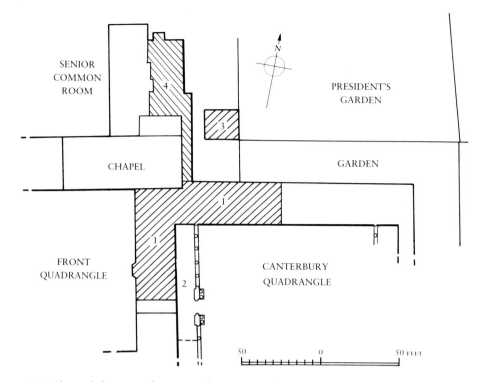

59. Plan of the President's Lodgings. (1) the Lodgings. (2) West range of cloister with Long Gallery above. (3) President's Kitchen 1643–1840, with former garden walls. (4) President's Kitchen 1840–1954

accounts.[6] On the ground floor the President gained a new kitchen, larder, and entry. Immediately above these was a new 'Great Room' or 'Great Chamber', today the 'Great Parlour' (Fig. 60). The accounts show that this was enlarged while under construction. Labourers were paid 'for beating downe the partition of the greate Roome when it was enlarged and carrying away the rubbish', and a carpenter received 10s. 'for remooving the partition of the President's greate Roome to enlarge it Eastwards'. From the way the fireplace blocks up a window in the north wall (still visible externally), it can be deduced that the room was originally only two windows wide, but was extended to take in a third. It is lined with early seventeenth-century panelling ornamented with Ionic pilasters, and there is a decorative overmantel with Laud's arms displayed in a cartouche (Fig. 61). The ceiling and the principal doorway (Fig. 62) both incorporate a well-known pattern of interlocking shapes derived from one of the plates in Serlio's *Architettura*.[7] The whole forms an excellent example of the decorative taste of the 1630s, in which the grosser forms of Jacobean mannerism have begun to yield to orthodox classical influence. The panelling was made by the Oxford joiner David Woodfield

[6] See esp. pp. 41–4 and 55–8.
[7] S. Serlio, *Architettura* (Venice, 1619), lib. iv, fo. 194ᵛ.

60. The Great Parlour of the President's Lodgings. *Above*, photographed in 1936.
Below, in 1986 (*Sir John Kendrew*)

INCHES 12 6 0   1   2   3   4   5   6 FEET

61. The chimney-piece in the Great Parlour (from Henry Tanner's *English Interior Woodwork*, 1902)

for £52, plus £3 for the doorway.[8] The overmantel was not charged for separately, and was no doubt included in the total.[9] It was presumably in

[8] For Woodfield (*c*.1597–1668) see M. Toynbee and P. Young, *Strangers in Oxford* (1973), p. 49. Another possible work of his is the panelling made for the Globe Room at the rear of the Reindeer Inn at Banbury in or about 1637, which has features in common with the St John's Great Parlour. It is illustrated by H. Tanner, *English Interior Woodwork* (1902) pl. XXXIII and by J. A. Gotch, *Early Renaissance Architecture in England* (1901), pl. XLIX.

[9] There are no payments in the accounts for painter's work either in the President's Lodgings or

INCHES 12   6   0   1   2   3   4   5   6 FEET

62. The doorway in the Great Parlour (from Henry Tanner's *English Interior Woodwork*, 1902)

this room that in September 1661 President Baylie, as Vice-Chancellor, entertained the Chancellor, the Earl of Clarendon, to dinner.[10]

elsewhere in the Canterbury Quadrangle, but many layers of paint were found when the panelling in the Great Parlour was stripped in 1963. According to Tanner, writing in 1902 (op. cit. 6), the woodwork was then 'all varnished and elaborately gilded' (probably in a manner similar to the Victorian pelmets surviving in store), but prior to 1963 it was covered with a dark yellowish paint, and in 1963 it was painted white, the colour of the earliest layer identified (Muniments, lxxxi. 55).

[10] A. Wood, *Life and Times*, ed. A. Clark, Oxford Historical Society i (1891), 414.

The joiner Woodfield also wainscotted the parlour at a cost of £30. This was a ground-floor room, almost certainly the present dining room, which was known in the eighteenth century as the 'fore-parlour'. The sum expended implies workmanship of some elaboration, and the chimney-piece was ornamented with a 'frett'.[11] Other workmanship by Woodfield included 'making a dore into the Chamber adjoining' the Great Chamber and 'carvinge the President's staire case'. The staircase itself (Fig. 63) was made by William Hudson, carpenter, under an agreement dated 4 April 1632, but a turner supplied the 'bannisters', of which there were (and are) twenty-seven (twenty-two whole and ten halves), and Woodfield made a 'Closett under the greate Staires' and a 'Portall going in to the Chappell'.[12] The Chapel is immediately to the north of the staircase, and there has been direct access to it from the Lodgings at least since 1573, when, in consideration of the 'straight rometh' in the Lodgings, the College allowed the President to appropriate the vestry.[13] The existing internal Gothick sash window lighting the closet or vestry beneath the stairs (Fig. 63) was made in 1764–5.[14] On the west side facing the Front Quadrangle a new stone entrance doorway to the President's hall was constructed in 1632–5 to match the new doorway leading to the Canterbury Quadrangle. The Founder's arms which surmount the broken pediment were carved by John Jackson, who also carved the arms of Archbishop Laud over the doorway to the quadrangle[15] (Fig. 44).

An important feature of the enlarged Lodgings was the Long Gallery, which occupies most of the space over the western cloister. A Long Gallery was a common feature of the grander English houses of the time, and there are several in Cambridge colleges. In Oxford the only other example was at Merton, where a 'College Gallery' is mentioned as the scene of a banquet in 1629. It appears to have formed part of the Warden's Lodgings, and was probably situated on the upper floor of the Fellows' Quadrangle, built by Sir Henry Savile in 1610, but has since been divided up[15a]. The accounts of 1632–5 record no significant expenditure on the interior of the gallery at St John's. Its ceiling appears always to have been unornamented, and the existing panelling probably dates from the eighteenth century.

Although the enlarged Lodgings were structurally complete by the end of 1635, their embellishment evidently continued, either at Laud's expense or at that of Richard Baylie, who succeeded Juxon as President in

[11] Building Accounts, pp. 55, 57.
[12] Building Accounts, pp. 36, 55.
[13] College Register, i, fo. 104ᵛ.
[14] Acc. V. B1, carpenter's bill, 1764–5.
[15] Building Accounts, p. 60. The legs of the bird forming the crest were supplied in iron (p. 48).
[15a] G. C. Brodrick, *Memorials of Merton College* (Oxford Hist. Soc., 1885), p. 75, n. 2. For information about the Merton gallery I am indebted to Dr J. R. L. Highfield.

63. The staircase in the President's Lodgings, made in 1632 at Laud's expense (*Country Life*). The Gothick sash-window was made in 1764–5

1633. Some sections of wooden moulding, with well-carved lions' masks and the date 1637, were in the nineteenth century made up into pelmets for the windows of the Great Parlour. Now in store, they are presumably relics of some decorative feature executed in 1637. Another item that cannot be identified in the accounts of 1632–5, though obviously a work of the 1630s, is a very small attic room over the Long Gallery immediately behind the great western pediment. Measuring only about ten feet square, it is completely panelled in a style similar to the Great Parlour, with ornamental chimney-piece and dentilled cornice (Fig. 64). However, the woodwork fits the room awkwardly, and was very likely brought here from some other part of the Lodgings.

As enlarged in 1632–5, the Lodgings therefore formed an L-shaped

64. Chimney-piece in attic room of President's Lodgings

dwelling with access from both quadrangles as well as from the President's close or yard to the north (Fig. 59). Within the north range the easternmost room on the first floor (probably then as now the principal bedchamber) extended over the westernmost of the commoners' rooms on the ground floor. In order to bring the latter room under his control President Baylie rented it from the College from 1662/3 onwards, and successive Presidents continued to pay £5 a year for it until 1775, when the College resolved 'that the Room under the great Chamber be added to the Lodgings and . . . be enjoy'd by the President and his Successors, clear of all Charges and Payments whatsoever.'[16]

The acquisition of this room was followed in 1778–80 by extensive internal alterations for President Dennis which included the redecoration in elegant late Georgian style of the fore-parlour (now the dining-room) in the old part of the Lodgings.[17] It was probably about this time that the curved back staircase in the Canterbury wing was constructed. The secondary staircase from the hall up to what is now the President's study

[16] *Computus Annuus*, 1662/3 onwards; College Register, vii, 486, 7 Oct. 1775: 'great chamber' must here mean 'Principal Bed Chamber'.
[17] Acc. V.B1, carpenter's bills, 1778–80.

and the adjoining bedroom was built in 1797–8. It was designed and executed by the carpenter-architect James Pears who was also responsible for the Holmes Building.[18]

Although a kitchen had been constructed in 1632–5 at the west end of the Canterbury wing of the Lodgings, it cannot easily have been fitted into the space available, and its situation immediately beneath the Great Chamber was potentially a source of annoyance: hence the expenditure of 7s. 8d. on 'counter-lathing the Kitchin, Larder & Entry to keep the steame from the greate Roome'.[19] In order to avoid these inconveniences a new kitchen was built in 1642–3.[20] The engravings of Loggan (1675) and Williams (1733) show it as a square detached building of two storeys standing in the President's yard about twenty-five feet to the north of the Canterbury Quadrangle (Fig. 59). On the east side two substantial chimney-stacks proclaimed its primary function, and on the upper floor there were several rooms for servants. In this building the food for the President's household was prepared until about 1840, when President Wynter had it pulled down as an obstruction to the view from his windows, 'most unsightly in appearance, and quite out of harmony with the College buildings'.[21] In its place he constructed a new kitchen abutting on the east side of the Senior Common Room, complete with dairy, larder, and housekeeper's room. The food was conveyed to the dining room, some thirty-five yards distant, by means of a passageway outside the east end of the chapel.

The Lodgings themselves were little altered in the course of the nineteenth century, but in President Wynter's time (1828–71) the Georgian 'fore-parlour' on the ground floor became the dining-room and the Great Room, hitherto used as, and generally referred to as, the dining-room, became the drawing-room or Great Parlour, by which latter name it is still known.

After the Second World War President Wynter's kitchen was no longer used, and in 1954 it was demolished (with the exception of the porch) to make way for an extension of the Senior Common Room. A new and smaller kitchen was fitted up in the old position beneath the Great Parlour. In 1949 the ground-floor room annexed to the Lodgings in 1775, and known as the Morning Room, was divided up under the direction of Sir Edward Maufe in order to provide a cloakroom for President Poole's servants.[22] In 1938, during the presidency of Sir Cyril Norwood, Maufe

[18] College Register, viii, 44.
[19] Building Accounts, p. 56.
[20] *Victoria County History of Oxfordshire*, iii. 262.

[21] Printed statement by President Wynter of his expenditure, 1867 (Muniments, lxxxvi. G.2).
[22] Muniments, lxxxi. 47. This room is now (1987) about to be restored to its former shape.

had removed the fine marble chimney-pieces inserted in the fireplaces in the Great Parlour and Long Gallery by President Holmes (1728–48) and had substituted stone ones for his own designing.[23] In 1969 the insertion of a lift at the west end of the Canterbury wing of the Lodgings necessitated certain alterations in that area, and provided an opportunity to straighten out the internal wall on the north side of the lobby between the great Parlour and the Long Gallery, which had hitherto been awkwardly oblique in plan.

[23] In his will President Holmes bequeathed to the College: 'the marble chimney pieces put up by me in the President's Lodgings' (College Register, vii. 208).

5.

The Rooms in the Canterbury Quadrangle

WHEN the Canterbury Quadrangle, was complete, Archbishop Laud wrote to the College to say how he wanted the new buildings he had erected to be used. After dealing with the library and the President's Lodgings, he went on to enumerate the additions he had made to the residential accommodation of the College: on the north side, 'five double chambers, one single, and three cocklofts [*i.e. attic rooms*], with studies . . . as allsoe all that I have built at [the] west end of the Library, as well belowe as above staires, towards the old quadrangle, being three double chambers and one single: as likewise that [chamber] upon the ground [floor] on the east end under the Library, for soe much as enlarges the chamber that was there by twenty foote'. All these were to be 'let out unto such Commoners from tyme to tyme as shall live within the Colledge . . . according to the rates usually sett upon chambers of like goodnes in other colledges of that University'.[1] Thereafter, for over two hundred years, the Canterbury Quadrangle formed the exclusive preserve of commoners, no fellow or scholar being allowed to occupy rooms there until 1867, when the reformed Governing Body decided to make them available to all members of the College alike.[2]

The rooms mentioned in Laud's letter are enumerated in a document dated 1 January 1635/6 fixing the rates at which they were to be let to their occupants.[3] On the north side there were, on the first floor, two double chambers and one single one, to each of which was attached a 'cockloft', and on the ground floor three double chambers. The best room, rated at £7 a year, is described as 'the Middle [*i.e. first-floor*] chamber on the North side with the Cockloft looking towarde the Grove [*i.e. the garden*]'. The second-best room, rated at £6, was the next one westwards on the first floor. The remaining rooms were rated at £5, £4, or £3 each, according to size or situation. The identification of these

[1] College Register, iii, 142. Laud's wishes were formally ratified by the College in a document bearing the corporate seal and that of the Visitor (lxxxv, H. 1), of which there are copies in the College Register iii. 144–5 and in the Visitor's register of documents relating to the College (now FN II, A.7).

[2] College Register x, 50. The Chaplain was, however, provided with a chamber on the south side of the quadrangle (A. Wood, *The History of the Colleges and Halls in the University of Oxford* (1674) ed. J. Gutch (1786), p. 548, n. 46).

[3] College Register, iii, 147.

rooms is complicated by the absence of any plan of the quadrangle earlier in date than 1888, and by much subdivision and rearrangement at various times. Moreover it was a peculiarity of the quadrangle that on both north and south sides the easternmost room on the ground floor was accessible only through the adjoining set, having no external doorway of its own: the existing doorways at the north and south ends of the eastern cloister date from 1887 and 1965, respectively. At first-floor level on the north side there was a doorway between the easternmost room and the Laudian Library,[4] but as the library was kept locked the occupant of that room must normally have reached it through the adjoining chamber. In fact it is clear that these three rooms were originally joined with the adjacent ones to form unusually generous double sets. All three were subdivided to provide studies, but the partition survives only in what is now room C 4,2. The double set rated at £7 must therefore have comprised what are now rooms C3,2 and C 4,3, together with a cockloft, while the £6 set consisted of room C 2,2 with an adjoining study or studies and a cockloft. On the first floor each chamber was lit on the side facing the quadrangle by two two-light windows, but on the ground floor by one single and one two-light window, an arrangement reflecting the fenestration of the Elizabethan range on the other side of the quadrangle. Here (as in the medieval Front Quadrangle) the single-light windows were designed to light studies partitioned off from the main chamber. However, in the north range of the Canterbury Quadrangle there seems to have been no correlation between single-light windows and studies, although in rooms C 2,1 and C 3,1 mortice-holes in the overhead beams indicate long narrow spaces running from front to rear which may (as at Wadham College) have served as studies.[5] On the south side of the quadrangle there were already four double chambers beneath the library.[6] To these Laud added three double chambers to the west of the library staircase, each with two studies (Figs. 77–8), one single chamber nearby, and the additional chamber beneath the east end of the Old Library, which, like the corresponding chamber on the north side, served to 'enlarge' the adjoining room, to which it was joined.

Internally, little now remains on the ground floor of the original

---

[4] See above, p. 73.

[5] See the plan in T. G. Jackson, *Wadham College, Oxford* (1893), pp. 124–5.

[6] The main partitions between these four chambers remained in place until they were removed to convert the rooms into the Lower Library in 1975–6 (see Fig. 77). In the course of the work evidence was found in the soffits of two of the windows in the south wall that at some time they had been enlarged from single to twin lights, and it would appear that one rear window in every room had originally been of one light only, as in the front wall towards the quadrangle. There is no evidence in the building accounts of 1632–5 to suggest that the enlargement was done then. Photographs of the exposed soffits are in the College Muniments, lxxxii. 277.

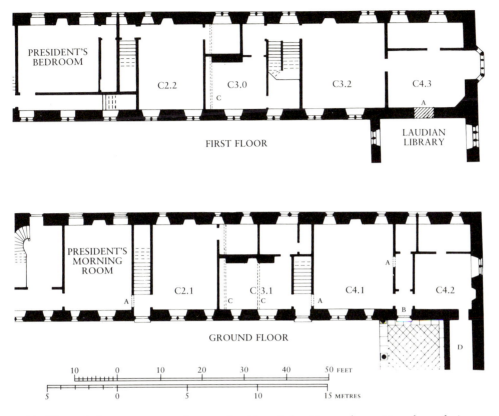

65. Plan of the rooms on the north side of the Canterbury Quadrangle in about 1900 (with the present numbering)

A. Original doorways blocked up   B. Doorway formed in 1887

C. Position of former partitions   D. Otranto Passage

arrangements. By the eighteenth century 'chumming' or sharing was no longer regarded as acceptable, and every set was reorganized to provide a sitting-room and bedroom for a single occupant. Georgian architraves, wainscot, and chimney-pieces were introduced, and in many cases remain to the present day, even in those rooms that have been converted to other purposes, such as the Lower Library (formed in 1975–6 out of the original four sets), the former Undergraduates' Library (now Room C4,1), and the New Seminar Room (from 1889 to 1975 the Junior Common Room). Many of these eighteenth-century fittings probably date from the 1740s, when it was decreed that anyone fitting up a chamber 'in a handsome and durable manner' at his own expense should be entitled to recover four-fifths of the outlay from his successor, and an estimate was obtained of the cost of wainscotting eight chambers in the Canterbury Quadrangle.[7] There were further changes in 1829, when the College decided that three of the rooms in the quadrangle were to be divided into two sets.[8] It was probably at this date that room C 3,1 was subdivided so as to provide bedrooms for itself and the adjoining room C 2,1.

On the north side of the quadrangle, however, two rooms on the first floor (C 2,2 and C 3,2) retain early seventeenth-century panelling of high quality (Figs. 66,67). In room C 3,2 the panelling is embellished with fluted Ionic pilasters, and in both the chimney-pieces have decorative overmantels. The mannerist detailing is similar in character to that in the Great Parlour of the President's Lodgings and must date from the 1630s or 1640s. The ceilings are identically moulded, indicating that both rooms must have been fitted up at approximately the same time. In College folklore these two rooms have been associated since the late nineteenth century with the royal entertainment of 1636, when it is supposed that they were occupied by King Charles and Prince Rupert, but there is not the slightest evidence to substantiate this figment of Victorian romanticism.[9] In fact it is unlikely that the panelling was there in 1636, for in the building accounts there is no reference to the wainscotting of rooms other than those in the Lodgings. Unless Laud himself commissioned the panelling some time after the completion of the quadrangle (which seems unlikely), it was presumably introduced by one of the commoners who rented the rooms. Although the names of the occupants of the Canterbury Quadrangle are known from the College accounts, it is not normally possible to relate them to individual rooms. The two panelled rooms are, however, an exception. During the years 1642–6, when Oxford was a Royalist stronghold, many colleges were partly taken over by courtiers. Christ Church housed the King and his household, Merton the Queen. At St John's three rooms in the Canterbury Quadrangle were requisitioned by 'the Earl of Devonshire'.[10] This was William Cavendish, fourth Earl of Devonshire, who had been with the King in York in June 1642, and who is known to have attended the Parliament convened at Oxford in January 1644 before going overseas 'to wait for peace at home'.[11] Those who

[7] College Register, vii, 137, 23 July 1742; Muniments, lxxxi. 13.

[8] College Register, viii, 401, 3 July 1829.

[9] 'Very modern fiction' was how W. H. Hutton (then a fellow of the College) described it in 1909 (*Oxford and Cambridge delineated by Hanslip Fletcher* (1909), 130).

[10] *Computus Annuus* 1642/3, 1643/4. In 1643/4 the Earl's butler was paid 2s. by the College 'for looking to our beere'.

[11] W. Kennet, *A Sermon Preach't at the Funeral of the Rt. Hon. William, Duke of Devonshire* (1708), 81.

made way for the earl were Sir Henry Sedley, Lord Sherard, and John Lewknor, all of whom had matriculated in 1639.[12] The rooms occupied by Sir Henry Sedley and Lord Sherard were those rated at £7 and £6, respectively, and it is possible to identify their original occupants in 1636 as, in the case of Sir Henry's room, John Herne sharing with William Thomas, and in that of Lord Sherard, George Grigg who shared it first with Michael Miller and then with Thomas Cave. In 1644/5 the Earl of Devonshire was succeeded by a new set of Royalists. John Dutton of Sherborne in Gloucestershire, and MP for that county, described by Anthony Wood as 'one of the richest . . . men in England',[13] took over the two best rooms, Sir Robert Croke, an Oxfordshire gentleman who had recently been knighted by the King, moved into Mr Lewknor's and Mr Fretwell's chambers, priced at £5 and £4, and 'Mr. Howard' (probably one of the sons of Thomas Howard, Earl of Berkshire), those of Mr Scudamore and Mr Gosnell, priced at £4 and £5 respectively.[14]

As the Bursar sadly noted in his accounts, these 'Noble gentlemen imploied in the King's Service', were not to be relied upon to pay the rent of their rooms.[15] But John Dutton proved to be a generous tenant. In 1645, at a time when St John's was in dire financial straits, he first lent the College £40, and then forgave the debt. In gratitude, the President and fellows gave him the use, rent-free, of the rooms he inhabited in the Canterbury Quadrangle. They were described as 'the two upper chambers in the New Quadrangle on the north side next unto the Grove', an ambiguous phrase which, however interpreted, must include at least the eastern of the two panelled rooms.[16] Either the Earl of Devonshire or John Dutton could, therefore, have paid for the panelling, and of the two the wealthy Dutton is the more probable. But it may be thought unlikely that either of these Cavaliers would have laid out money embellishing his temporary quarters in an Oxford college, and if so the evidence points to Sir Henry Sedley and Lord Sherard, the only commoners to have been in sole occupation of the rooms in question between 1636 and the Civil War.

Despite over three centuries of continuous occupation by a succession of junior and latterly senior members of the College, the two panelled rooms still look much as they must have done in the 1640s. At some time room C 2,2 has, however, been reduced in size by about two feet, apparently to enlarge the adjoining study, and this has resulted in the slight asymmetry apparent in the ceiling. There have been more drastic changes

---

[12] J. Foster, *Alumni Oxonienses 1500–1714* (1891), 912, 1332, 1346.
[13] A. Wood, *Fasti Oxonienses*, ed. P. Bliss, ii (1820), 42.
[14] *Computus Annuus* 1644/5.
[15] *Computus Annuus* 1644/5, fo. 39ᵛ.
[16] College Register, iii, 362, Dec. 1645.

66. Interior of Room C2, 2 (*Country Life*). Since this photograph was taken in 1929, a window has been opened up to the left of the fireplace

67. Interior of Room C3, 2 (*Country Life*), photographed in 1929

in the inner room C 4,3 overlooking the garden. In 1937 it was rearranged for W. C. Costin by Edward Maufe, who removed the original study partitioned off across its north side as in the room below.[17] In 1982 it was separated from its panelled neighbour, access being provided by a spiral staircase contrived in the lobby between rooms C 4,1 and 2.

[17] Bursary File 220, fos. 73, 121.

68. A doorway in the Canterbury Quadrangle

6.

Repair and Restoration
1636–1986

NEITHER during the sieges of Oxford in 1642–6 nor subsequently under the Commonwealth and Protectorate was any damage apparently done to the Canterbury Quadrangle. No hostile hand sought to deface the emblems of royalty and prelacy, and the statues of the King and Queen survived unscathed, either because they were deliberately concealed or because they proved unsaleable as scrap metal.[1]

During the last two centuries the quadrangle has been affected by three principal causes of dilapidation: natural decay of the stonework, aggravated by atmospheric pollution; fissure of the Bletchingdon marble columns; and the instability of the battlemented parapets, which were provided with insufficient structural support.

By the middle of the nineteenth century the wall surfaces had already begun to assume that leprous appearance which results from the flaking and blistering characteristic of the Headington stone of which they were built. This is apparent in the earliest photograph of the quadrangle, taken by W. H. Fox Talbot in 1843 (Fig. 69), and the progressive deterioration of the stonework is attested by many later photographs (Fig. 70).

The first collapse was due to a great gale in February 1661/2. Anthony Wood records:

At St. John's College three single chimneys belonging to the chambers under the library and running up on the south side of the same were blowne downe and falling upon the roof beat into the library with great losse: besides this, half of the battlements over the east Cloister there blowed downe, as also severall trees in their grove.[2]

The repair of the damage would have been recorded in the *Computus Annuus* for 1661/2, which has not been preserved, but evidence was found in 1887–8 that the battlements affected were those over the southern half of the east cloister. A new wall-plate had been inserted here to give better support to the restored parapet and the upper copings had been renewed in Headington stone.[3]

---

[1] See above, p. 38.
[2] A. Wood, *Life and Times*, i, ed. A. Clark, Oxford Historical Society (1891), 432.

[3] J. J. Stevenson's record of the repairs effected in 1888 (Muniments, lxxxii. 307), p. 6.

69. The earliest photograph
of the Canterbury Quad-
rangle, made by W. H. Fox
Talbot in 1843 (*Science
Museum, London*)

70. The east frontispiece in
1907, showing the con-
dition of the stonework

No further structural failure occurred until the Easter Vacation of 1887, when about thirty feet of the parapet on the north side of the Old Library fell into the quadrangle and it was considered expedient to take down another thirty feet which were in imminent danger of falling. Doubts were also felt about the stability of much of the parapet over the east cloister, and this in turn was dismantled on professional advice. A general survey and repair was clearly called for, but the College was suffering from the effects of the agricultural depression, and lacked the means to meet its ordinary running costs, let alone an expensive programme of restoration. Luckily an old member of the College, J. J. Moubray of Naemoor, Perthshire (1857–1928), came to the rescue with a gift of £1,500.[4] The architect appointed was J. J. Stevenson (1832–1908). Although he no doubt owed the job to the fact that he was the brother-in-law of the Bursar, T. S. Omond, for whom he had recently designed a house in the Banbury Road (No. 29, now part of St Anne's College), Stevenson was exceptionally well qualified for the delicate task of restoring the Canterbury Quadrangle. He was a founder member of the Society for the Protection of Ancient Buildings and a determined opponent of the sort of wholesale and insensitive restoration that was so common in the nineteenth century. 'I believe', he wrote, 'that a large amount of the renewal of the stone surfaces of Oxford buildings which has been done lately has been unnecessary, so far as stability was concerned'.[5] At St John's the general principle he followed was 'that nothing should be restored unless it was necessary on account of the stability of the building'. Whenever possible the old stone was retained or re-used. Thus in the case of leaning parapets Stevenson would have them carefully dismantled and rebuilt after defective wall-plates had been replaced by brickwork or concrete, and considerable ingenuity was used to accomplish this with the minimum of disturbance to the masonry still in place.[6] Stevenson wrote:

On the same principle the carvings, even though decayed, have been left. The committee [*consisting of the President, the Vice-President, the Bursar, and Mr Moubray*] desired that one of each of the various types of carvings should be renewed in order to perpetuate the record, and occasion was taken of some of the carvings having been completely defaced or broken in the fall of the parapet to do this. . . .

Another principle followed was that the new work should shew itself to be new work, and the new carvings are consequently modern in style, no attempt being made to reproduce the want of anatomy and rude modelling of the old.

[4] College Register, x, 245, 248, 252, 254, 260–1; Muniments, lxxxi. 25, 29, 30. Moubray was elected to an Honorary Fellowship in 1889.

[5] Stevenson's record, p. 2.
[6] Ibid. 3–6.

The new work is also shewn by the new carvings being in Milton stone and the ashlar in Bath stone, not in Headington which cannot now be got.

When the old carvings were partly broken I have had them mended instead of wholly renewed. In parts of the carvings of the portico[s] this has been done in cement.

I believe the result of carrying out these principles has been that the old building remains as an historical record, and that it is more interesting and picturesque in appearance than if it had been more extensively renewed. Continual watchfulness was required to carry them out, the masons preferring total renewal.[7]

To give effect to these principles careful day-to-day supervision was essential, and as clerk of works Stevenson recommended a young man in his office called F. W. Troup (1859–1941).[8] 'Troup', he later wrote, 'was a good draughtsman and . . . in assisting me at St. John's College, Oxford, he shewed himself a good archaeologist'. Where Troup especially demonstrated his 'archaeological' ability was in recovering the pattern of the original painted decoration on the leaden rainwater heads and downpipes. By 1888 this had been almost obliterated by weathering, but 'sufficient remained to make an accurate restoration', despite the fact that there were 'traces of a later pattern' overlaying the original one.[9]

In addition to repairing the stonework, Stevenson had to deal with the roof of the Old Library. As built in 1596–8 this consisted of a series of closely spaced spars or rafters without any principals, purlins, or tie-beams. The collars which framed one spar to another were placed too high to prevent the latter from spreading at the feet (Fig. 71). As a result the vertical posts rising from the wall-plates were leaning outwards, and, more seriously, the north wall of the library itself had been pushed out of the perpendicular to the extent of two to four and a half inches. In 1837 this roof, then in bad repair, had been overlaid by a new roof of deal with conventional principals and scissor-beams, so that the original roof was relieved of the weight of the stone slates which it had hitherto supported.[10] But as this new outer roof itself lacked any tie-beams, it too was spreading and contributing to the displacement of the wall below. Stevenson effectively arrested this movement by inserting a series of iron tie-rods, supported in the centre by vertical 'chains' attractively designed in such a way as to 'rather improve than injure the appearance of the Old Library inside'.[11]

---

[7] Ibid. 2.

[8] For Troup see N. Jackson, *F. W. Troup, Architect 1859–1941* (Building Centre Trust 1985).

[9] Stevenson's record, p. 8.

[10] *Computus Annuus* 1838; Muniments, lxxxi. 17; cf. Stevenson's record, p. 3.

[11] Stevenson's record, p. 3; letter to the Bursar, 10 Jan. 1888 (Muniments, lxxxi. 25).

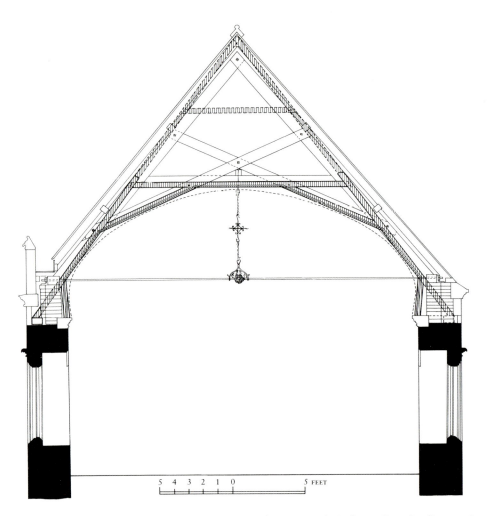

71. Section of the roof of the Old Library. The original timbers (hatched) remain up to the lower collar. Their destroyed upper portions are shown in broken lines. They are overlaid by the new roof (unhatched) of 1837. The iron ties inserted in 1888 are seen below, restraining the roof from spreading further. The profile of the former plaster ceiling is shown by a broken line.

When the work was completed Stevenson and Troup drew up an exemplary record of all that had been done for preservation in the College records.[12] It was, he concluded, 'a matter for congratulation that unlike other Colleges in Oxford [St John's had been] handed on to posterity with its venerable appearance and its old features remaining'.

Although J. J. Moubray's generosity eventually enabled the College to extend Stevenson's operations to the Front Quadrangle, nothing was done to the garden front of the library beyond invisible repairs to the par-

[12] Muniments, lxxxii. 307, a large folio volume with plans, sections, diagrams, and photographs.

72. Angel holding a shield with the arms of J. J. Moubray, the benefactor who paid for the repair of the Canterbury Quadrangle in 1888: a Victorian carving in the string-course on the south side of the quadrangle, photographed in 1907

apet, which was stabilized by replacing the decayed wall-plate with brickwork, inserted from within so as to avoid any disturbance to the masonry. However, the stonework continued to decay, its natural degeneration aggravated by a luxuriant growth of ornamental creepers, for whose support the wall-surface was pock-marked with metal fastenings (Fig. 73).

By the early twentieth century it was obvious that the repair of the garden front could no longer be postponed, and in 1909 the College consulted the Society for the Protection of Ancient Buildings (with which it had previously been in touch in 1887–8). The Society recommended the employment of Harry Redfern, an architect who specialized in the restoration of ancient buildings and who had been Stevenson's partner during the last ten years of the latter's life.[13] After two inspections (one of them in the company of Troup, now an architect in independent practice, and William Weir, an architect associated with the SPAB), Redfern reported that the masonry in general was stable, but that the plinth, the cornice, the parapet, and other salient architectural features 'have perished badly', and that there were 'fissures and displacements' in the oriel windows, one of which 'had lost all support from its corbels', which were 'broken through'. His policy, like Stevenson's, was that 'no new stone whatsoever

---

[13] College Register, x, 437–8. For Redfern see obituaries in *Builder* 178 (1950), 669 and *RIBA Journal* 57 (1950), 245.

73. The garden front as it was in 1910

74. The garden front in 1986

should be inserted where an existing one can be made to continue its duty, with such help as may be given by bronze bolts or cramps or additional bonding'. In this way the garden front—'surely one of the most beautiful pieces of architecture in England'—could 'be given a new lease of life'. The Governing Body accepted his advice and the work was carried out under his direction in the years 1910–11.[14] Redfern himself explained his methods to the Royal Archaeological Institute when that society visited the College in the summer of 1910:

He described the process as being similar to that employed by a dentist for the stopping of a decayed tooth. They found when the creeper had been removed that the state of the stone was very bad indeed in places. . . . The original stone had been obtained from the local quarries at Headington. This appears to have been at first of a good quality; but as the demand increased the stone was taken from inferior strata. In addition it often happened, as at St. John's, that it was not laid with regard to its proper bed. As a consequence of this, as well as owing to the injurious atmospheric conditions, the greater number of old Oxford buildings are to-day scarcely ever entirely free from scaffolding. Mr. Redfern said the decayed parts on the garden front were first cut out; this had to be done most carefully as the building would not stand hammering. When the sound stone was reached the surface was covered by a frontal wall of hand-made roofing tiles bonded into it, which were fixed and faced with lias lime. The broken corbels under the oriel window were drilled through from front to back in situ and copper bolts inserted. Finally the whole surface was repeatedly coated with baryta water.[15] The colour, which is not at first in harmony with old work, is expected to become like it in from five to ten years. This process enables Mr. Redfern to claim that not a single stone has been removed and not a single new one inserted.[16]

Between them Stevenson and Redfern had given the Canterbury Quadrangle a new lease of architectural life. But not a long one. A building whose walls are a patchwork of decaying stone and tiles covered with cement is of doubtful validity, both structurally and aesthetically. There is a point beyond which the attempt to preserve the workmanship of the original builder becomes futile. Once every ashlar has lost most of its dressed surface, every moulding its original profile, and every carving its detail, there is nothing left worth preserving. Moreover the original design cannot be appreciated properly if all its principal features are so blurred by decay that the voids are no longer framed by clear-cut solids and the emphasis intended by decoration is lost. To nineteenth-century taste, which (at any rate in Oxford) much preferred the picturesque to the formal, and chose to hide so many distinguished buildings behind a

[14] Muniments, lxxxi. 32.
[15] An alkaline wash which formed a 'water-proof glaze' on the surface of the stone.
[16] *Archaeological Journal*, lxvii (1910), 350–1.

rampant growth of vegetation, this was perfectly acceptable. But twentieth-century taste, though by no means insensitive to the charms of picturesque decay, has shown more interest in strictly architectural qualities, and has accepted that accurate restoration in new stonework may be legitimate as well as inevitable.

In the case of the Canterbury Quadrangle the necessity of replacement had already been recognized in 1905, when five of the columns (three in the west cloister and two in the east) were found to be in a dangerous state and, together with their bases, were replaced in Portland stone on Stevenson's advice.[17] Although the white Portland stone did not match the grey Bletchingdon 'marble' of the original columns, it was probably the only suitable stone available from which to cut the seven-foot monoliths, and it would have satisfied Stevenson's principle that new work should be clearly identifiable as such. The columns had previously received attention in 1738, when they were underpinned and provided with new bases of Portland stone.[18] The eighteenth-century bases consist of two pieces of stone with a vertical joint, whereas those of 1905 are in one piece.

It was, however, not until 1922 that the replacement of decayed wall-surfaces in the Canterbury Quadrangle was at last authorized by the Governing Body, on the advice of the Oxford architect N. W. Harrison, with Redfern as consultant:[19]

During the Easter Vacation the western portico of the Canterbury Quadrangle was restored, and the two [pairs of] Ionic columns renewed. In the Long Vacation the eastern portico was thoroughly restored, including the Ionic columns, their capitals and carved pedestals, which have been replaced in new stone. The battlements on the west side of this Quadrangle and part of those on the south side have been replaced with new ones. The window-sills on the ground-floor on the north side were renewed. . . . The restoration has been carried out in Clipsham stone . . .[20]

The change in conservationist policy at St John's was the subject of favourable comment in the *Oxford Magazine*.[21] 'Cement patching', the writer (E. H. New) observed, 'provides a poor substitute for stone, and is particularly unpleasant where it is used to fill gaps in the carved mouldings and ornament'. Moreover it was liable to fall off, while the 'waterproof glaze' applied to the crumbling surface of the old stone not only looked unsightly but was apt to lead to further damage 'where moisture

[17] College Register, x, 394; Estates Committee Minutes, pp. 468–9. Stevenson's report on the columns has been lost.

[18] Transcript of bill (now apparently lost) filed under 'Laud's Quad' in W. H. Stevenson's MS Notes on the History of the College.

[19] College Register, x, 567, 571, 572.

[20] *College Record*, 1922–3.

[21] *Oxford Magazine*, 7 June 1923, p. 419.

has penetrated behind the protected surface and detached it in pieces'. 'The fact must be faced that old buildings will crumble, and that if something is not done the Canterbury Quadrangle of St. John's, together with many other precious buildings, will utterly perish, and will be known to future generations only from photographs and drawings.' What particularly commended the new policy to the *Oxford Magazine* was the sensitivity of the carving:

The quality of the new carving which takes the place of the almost obliterated panels and crumbling columns and capitals, may be more fully realised if it is compared with the restored southern face of the church of St. Mary Magdalen executed some years ago. The former, while it repeats the original design as faithfully as possible, has a vitality rarely found in copies, while the latter is comparatively cold and lifeless, however 'correct' in shape and style. The recent carving at St. John's was entrusted to Mr. E. S. Frith, a sculptor, of Chelsea, and we are permitted to publish his own account of his method. He writes: 'When the restoration was started I realized that there were two ways of approaching the work, viz., making a literal copy (this would have been difficult, as the stone was defaced) or endeavouring to enter into the spirit of the original craftsmen. A literal copy is a safe course, but it is usually lifeless, and it was the spontaneity of the work at St. John's that appealed to me and made it a pleasure to try and enter into the vision of the original craftsmen who thought in stone and saw only stone as a medium for their work. I was fortunate in having the services of Mr. Tanner, my carver, who feels the beauty of the original carvings as much as I . . . In restoration work a good deal must necessarily be conjectural. Before starting on the drawings of the reconstructed panels I spent a considerable time examining the better preserved carvings in the quadrangle, and as I worked it was a great satisfaction to find myself in entire sympathy with the men who had preceded me. I should have liked to carve the panels myself, but as my engagements did not permit me to do so Mr. Tanner, who has worked for us for many years, was entrusted with the work . . . and he carried it out with the assistance of a young carver.[22]

With Frith as carver, Benfield and Loxley as builders, and first Harrison (up to 1936) and then Maufe (from 1937 to 1960) as supervising architects, the College embarked on a programme of restoration which was to continue for over fifty years and which is still not fully accomplished today. The progress of the work may be summarized as follows:

1922–3   East and west frontispieces. Battlements on west side and west end of south range.

1925   West wall of west arcade stripped (revealing remains of blocked-up fifteenth-century doorways)[23] and re-rendered.

[22] *Oxford Magazine*, 22 Nov. 1923, pp. 128–9.
[23] Photographs in College Buildings Record, Muniments, lxxxii. 181.

1928   Battlements and all ornamental carving on garden front renewed.

1935–6   Renewal of battlements and refacing of most of walls on north and east sides. Sculptured frieze of arcades repaired.

1936–7   Repair of roofs damaged by death-watch beetle.

1949–50   North elevation facing President's garden, partial renewal of stonework.

1953   West side of quadrangle including frontispiece.

1958   East frontispiece.

1965–6   Upper part of south side of library, facing Trinity College.

1977–9   Replacement of all stonework on garden front not renewed in 1928.

At the present time the only areas where the original stonework remains substantially intact are the north face of the library, the lower part of the south face of the library, and the lower part of the south face of the north range, all of which have enjoyed some degree of protection from the prevailing south-west winds. The stone used throughout has been Clipsham, except on the south side of the library, where Casterton stone was found best to match the narrow coursing of the masonry of 1596–8. Although the north side of the library remains to be dealt with, a complete set of grotesques carved by Frith in 1956 is in store, so that when the time comes his handiwork will be seen on all four sides of the quadrangle. On the east and west sides no original carving now remains above the level of the main horizontal cornice, but below that level the original workmanship of the seventeenth-century carvers survives with careful repairs by Frith and his assistants. The painted decoration of the rainwater heads and down-pipes has been three times renewed since 1888: in 1935 and 1948 by W. H. Sharpington and again in 1974 by Messrs Campbell Smith.[24]

In 1935 the gravelled surface of the quadrangle was replaced by a lay-out of grass and York flagstones designed by Edward Maufe and paid for by a legacy of £500 from the late President, F. W. Hall.[25]

On the walls of the two cloisters there are four memorials. On either side of the western entrance there are stone panels carved with the names of members of the College killed in the first World War. These were designed by N. W. Harrison, then the College's architect.[26] On either side of the eastern entrance there are corresponding panels commemorating those who fell in the Second World War. The latter were designed by

---

[24] For Sharpington's work see College Register, xi, 96 and Muniments, lxxxi. 58; for Campbell Smith's, see Muniments, Cluttons' File BS 15.

[25] *College Record*, 1934, 1935.
[26] G.D. Register, 1914–21, p. 150.

Edward Maufe, with lettering cut by a sculptor called Angelo Coufato.[27] Maufe also designed the tablet to the memory of Sidney Ball, a fellow of the College who died in 1918. The inscription to the memory of W. C. Costin, fellow and President (d. 1970), was designed and executed in 1978 by David Kindersley and David Parsley.

[27] E. Maufe, 'Memories of St John's College, Oxford' (Muniments, lxxxi. 176), p. 7.

APPENDIX I

THE ICONOGRAPHY OF THE VIRTUES AND LIBERAL ARTS AS REPRESENTED IN THE SCULPTURED DECORATION OF THE CANTERBURY QUADRANGLE

Subject	Attributes[1]	Condition[2]
West Side (left to right)		
(1) Religion	Gothic churches and bibles	Nose restored
(2) Charity	Bare-breasted and accompanied by children with begging-bowls	Nose and breasts restored
(3) Hope	Anchors, the standard symbol of Hope (cf. St Paul, *Epistle to the Hebrews* 6:19)	Unrestored
(4) Faith	Crosses and altar-vessels	Nose restored
(5) Temperance	Vessels pouring water into wine	Nose and upper lip restored
(6) Fortitude	Pillars (recalling Samson's last heroic deed)	Nose restored
(7) Justice	Sword and scales	Nose restored
(8) Prudence	Snakes (cf. 'wise as serpents', *Matthew* 10:16) and mirrors (self-knowledge is the basis of prudence)	Nose and chin restored
East Side (left to right)		
(1) Learning	Scrolls and books	Face partly restored
(2) Astronomy	A cross-staff, an armillary sphere (right), a celestial globe (left), compasses, and books entitled: PTOLOMÆVS, ALFRAGANVS and MARC. MANILIVS. Ptolemy was a celebrated astronomer of the second century whose astronomical treatise was well known in the medieval West as the 'Almagest'.	

[1] The titles of the books are transcribed from the large-scale photographs of 1907 in the College archives (lxxxii.111).

[2] Based on a comparison between the large-scale photographs of 1907 and the sculpture after washing in 1986.

Subject	Attributes	Condition
	Alfraganus or al-Farghānī was a ninth-century Arab astronomer whose *Elements* was used in translation in the West. Marcus Manilius was a Roman senator and the author of a long astrological poem.	Face entirely renewed
(3) Geometry	She wears a mural crown and is flanked by geometrical and architectural instruments or tools and by books entitled, EVCLIDES, ARCHIMEDES, HYPSICLES and VITRUVIVS. The first three were celebrated Greek mathematicians. Vitruvius was the author of the only surviving Roman treatise on architecture.	Drapery and bridge of nose restored
(4) Music	Musical instruments and books entitled BOETIVS and ARIST: QUINT. The fifth-century Christian philosopher Boethius was the author of a treatise on Music and Aristides Quintilianus was a neo-Platonic writer on the theory of Music.	Tip of nose restored
(5) Arithmetic	Tables of numbers, counters, pens, and inkwells. Books entitled BAARLAM and DIAPHANTVS. Baarlam (or Bernardo of Seminara) was a fourteenth-century Calabrian monk who wrote a book on Greek methods of calculation entitled *Logistic*, of which editions were published in Strasburg in 1572 and Paris in 1600. Diophantus of Alexandria was a Hellenistic mathematician.	Nose restored

Subject	*Attributes*	*Condition*
(6) Logic	Snakes and books entitled: ARISTOTELES, AVERROES, SIMPLICIVS and IO: GRAMATICVS. Snakes had been an established attribute of Logic or Dialectic since Antiquity. Aristotle was the most celebrated philosopher of the Ancient World. Simplicius was a Greek philosopher of the sixth century who wrote a commentary on his work. Averroes was a famous Arab philosopher. John the Grammarian was a learned Patriarch of Constantinople in the ninth century.	Forehead and nose restored
(7) Rhetoric	*Caducei* (or 'Mercury's rods') and books entitled: DEMOSTHENES, CICERO, HERMOGENES and QVINTILIANVS. These were all celebrated rhetoricians of the Ancient World. The *caduceus* was the attribute of Mercury, the god of eloquence.	Nose restored
(8) Grammar	Keys and books entitled: MART. CAPELLA, PRISICIANS, and ÆL. DONATVS. Martianus Capella was the fifth-century author of an encyclopaedia of the seven liberal arts, in which Grammar figures prominently. Priscian was a celebrated Byzantine grammarian. Aelius Donatus was the author of a grammar and a well-known commentary on Vergil. Capella and others emphasize that grammar is the key to language and all the other arts.	Unrestored

PAINTED GLASS IN THE LIBRARY

THE east window of the Old Library contains panels of heraldic glass chiefly commemorating benefactors to the building or contents of the library in 1596–8. As the structure of the window was moved bodily eastwards when the library was extended by Archbishop Laud in 1633–5[1] there is every reason to suppose that the glass was removed with it without any rearrangement. The arms and inscriptions are given at length in Anthony Wood's *History of the Colleges and Halls*, written in the reign of Charles II, but subsequently revised before his death in 1695, and edited by Gutch in 1796.[2] His account agrees essentially both with a manuscript description of the glass made by Dr Michael Hutton in 1658 or 1659,[3] and with the glass as it exists today.

As listed by Hutton and Wood, the principal shields were those of:

Richard Warren, the Founder's nephew, who bequeathed £50.

William Craven, a Merchant Taylor, who gave £50.

The Founder, Sir Thomas White, whose family paid for the building of the window.

Queen Elizabeth I, the reigning sovereign at the time.

The Merchant Taylors' Company, which gave £100.

Robert Dowe, a Merchant Taylor, who gave £50, plus 50 nobles (£16 13s. 4d.) for books.[4]

Robert Berkeley, a gentleman commoner of the College, who gave £100 and laid one of the six foundation stones on 2 March 1596.[5]

Sir Thomas Tresham, who gave over a hundred books in 1598 and subsequent years.[6]

George Hangar, citizen and clothworker of London, who gave £10 to buy 'books of divinity'.

Of these nine shields, the first eight were all recorded by Hutton as being in the east window in 1658/9, but Hangar's was 'in a north window'. This is confirmed by Wood, according to whom it was in the third window from the east end on the north side, but by the end of the eighteenth century it had been transferred to a lower light of the east window, where it still remains. Scratched on it

[1] See above, p. 57.

[2] *Historia et Antiquitates Universitatis Oxoniensis* (1674), ii. 311; *The History and Antiquities of the Colleges and Halls in the University of Oxford*, ed. J. Gutch (1796), 552–4.

[3] Bodleian Library, MS Rawlinson B. 397, fos. 202–5.

[4] A letter from Dowe concerning his gift is in the College Muniments, x. 12. The inscription beneath his arms, as restored in 1986 on the auth-

ority of both Hutton and Wood, is in error in attributing to him a gift of only £15 instead of £50, the sum attested by both the College Register, iii, 93, and the Library Building Account.

[5] W. H. Stevenson and H. E. Salter, *Early History of St John's College* (1939), 295.

[6] For Tresham's gifts to the library see N. R. Ker, 'Oxford College Libraries in the Sixteenth Century', *Bodleian Library Record* 6 (1959), 512–15.

is the name of Christopher Wren (1591–1658), a fellow of the College who held the post of Librarian *c.*1616–20 and was later to be Dean of Windsor. Tresham's arms, listed by both Hutton and Wood, have disappeared apart from a fragment, but occupied another of the lower lights.

In addition the east window contains an oval portrait of the Founder, probably of seventeenth-century date, and a composite panel containing small representations of the arms of the Founder, of Archbishop Laud, dated 1633, of Bishop Juxon, dated 1636, and of Sir William Paddy (d. 1634), another benefactor to the College and Library. None of these was noted by Wood, but they were all seen by Gutch at the end of the eighteenth century.

No reference to the making of any of this glass is to be found either in the brief summary of expenditure on the new library in 1596–8 or in the accounts for Laud's works in 1633–6. In 1600/1, however, the College accounts record a payment of 4*s.* to 'the Glazier for mendinge the Hall windowes, the porter's Chamber windowes and setting up Mr. Alderman Craven his armes'.[7]

At some time in the eighteenth century the library windows were reglazed with rectangular instead of diamond quarries, and the arms in the east window must have been reset. The name 'J. Roberts glazier 1772' scratched on two pieces of glass in the east window suggests 1772 as the date when this happened, but the College accounts do not indicate any unusual expenditure on glazing at that time.

In 1986 all the panels were cleaned, repaired, and reset by Mr John Hayward. The inscriptions to the Warren, Craven, and Dowe panels, long missing, but recorded by Wood, were supplied by replicas, and the four small coats of arms were made up into a new panel together with a surviving fragment of the Tresham coat. At some time in the past the oval portrait of the Founder had been broken and replaced by a duplicate.[8] The fragments had, however, been preserved, and in 1986 it was found possible to repair the damage and restore the original portrait to its place in the central light, with a new border designed by Mr Hayward.

In the adjoining window on the south side of the Old Library, built in 1636,[9] there is a panel of the arms of William Laud as Archbishop of Canterbury, supported by two angels, with a landscape background. The date 1636 appears at the top. Cleaning by Mr Hayward has revealed this as a work of high quality which invites comparison with the contemporary glass in other Oxford colleges by Abraham and Bernard Van Linge.[10] The plumbing and glazing connected with the construction of this window was done by James Fletcher, but a total

[7] *Computus Annuus* 1601.

[8] In 1883 there were two portraits of the Founder in glass, one in the Library, the other in the President's Lodgings (*Proceedings of the Oxford Architectural and Historical Society*, NS, 4 (1880–5), 147). So it is possible that after the one in the Library was damaged, the one in the Lodgings was moved to take its place. For this and simi-

lar portraits in glass see Mrs R. L. Poole, 'Early Seventeenth-century Portraits in Stained Glass at Oxford', *Journal of the British Society of Master Glass-Painters*, 3 (1929–30).

[9] See above, p. 58.

[10] See M. Archer, 'English Painted Glass in the Seventeenth Century: The Early Work of Abraham van Linge', *Apollo*, 101 (1975).

payment to him of £4 18s. 'for glasse and leade used in the windows of the Gal-lerie [*i.e. the Laudian Library*] and the Bay Window in the olde Librarie'[11] can hardly include the cost of this decorative panel.

Standing in a frame in the Laudian Library there is a panel of painted glass representing a bay tree bearing on its branches shields of Laud's arms in his vari-ous academic and ecclesiastical preferments, culminating in the see of Canter-bury. This panel was formerly in the middle oriel window of the Laudian Library, whose central light was mutilated to accommodate it. It was not noticed by Wood in 1674, but he later mentions glass with the same arms as being 'in the middle window that looks eastward', and it remained there until 1928, when it was removed to enable the window to be restored to its proper form. It was pos-sibly at this time that some portions of the panel (other than the shields of arms) were apparently renewed with modern glass, but if so the accuracy of the resto-ration is attested by comparison with photographs taken in 1888.[12]

[11] PRO, SP 16/319, fo. 38 (76).
[12] Muniments, lxxxii. 51, 68–9.

APPENDIX III

TITLES PAINTED ON THE ENDS OF THE BOOK-PRESSES IN THE OLD LIBRARY

	Painted before 1746	*In use from 1746 onwards*
South Side	IVS CANONICVM	JUS CANON: & ANGLIC:
	IVS CIVILE	JUS CIVILE ROMAN:
	CASVISTA	MEDICINA & HIST: NAT:
	MEDICI	PHILOSOPH: & MATHEM:
	PHILOSOPHI	CLASSICI GR: & LAT:
	[*illegible*]	HIST: CIVIL: & CHRONOL:
	PHILOLOGI	ARCHAEOLOG: & GEOGRAPH:
	MISCELLANEI	POLYMATHIA
	VARII	PHILOLOGI
North Side	BIBLIA	BIBLIA & LIT: ORIENT:
	COMMENTATORES	S S PATRES.
	PATRES	COMMENT: BIBLICI
	SCOLASTICI	COMMENT: ECCLES: REF:
	CONTROVERSII	HIST: ECCLES: & CONCIL:
	COMMENT: REF: MCII(?)	THEOLOG: POLEMICA
	HISTORICI: CONCILIA	THEOLOG: SCHOLASTICA.
	VARII & MS^{TI}	THEOLOGIA MISCELL:
	VARII	VARII

APPENDIX IV

LETTERS FROM WILLIAM JUXON, PRESIDENT OF ST JOHN'S
COLLEGE, TO WILLIAM LAUD, BISHOP OF LONDON, MARCH
1631/2 (PRO, STATE PAPERS DOMESTIC, CHARLES I, VOL. 214,
fos. 38, 49)

My verie good Lord:

Wee have at length reviewd & examined all the Ingredients of the building which either our owne or our woorkmen's experience could call to mind, certaine I am wee have hipped nothing that may bee for charge considerable, and wee find, that the Peecing out of the Librarie 20 foote Eastward (which is the most it can neede) will cost neere upon the point of 120^l. That all the rest in consideration before, will cost within a little of 100^l more then the 3000 I conjectured it would. So that I am now confident, if your Lordshipp please to disburse 3200^l in the whole, the Quadrangle will be absolutely uniforme without the least eysoare more then the topps of the tunnelles of the Chimneys in the East range of the ould quadrangle, the Cloisters of the largest size that Art can allowe, & the Pillars of the best stone under marble growing in this part of England: And indeed seeing your Lordshipp was pleased to project a cloister, & of a forme not yet seene in Oxford, (for that under Jesus Coll: Librarie is a misfeatur'd thing)[1] I could wish (& so have cast it) a little extraordinarie charge might bee bestowed there, that that wherein wee are singular might bee eminent.

The 200 tunne of Timber given your Lordshipp (which was woorth 200^l in the Forrest) wee valew not in this accompt, but the Carriage & other charges about it wee doe, which amountes to 70^l; wee suppose likewise wee shall neede 200 tunn more (whereof wee have allreadie 85 tunn in the warrant) which wee valew with the Carriage, Fees & other charges at 30^s per tunn, in the whole 300^l, which also is part of the 3200^l. But where to provide that surplusage of timber, though a courser kind may serve the turn, as yet wee knowe not, but wee must seeke abroad; For as for Fifeild, Mr. White's necessities made him sell & take upp the moneyes ere the trees were fallen; and indeed, they would say heereafter when the want of timber there shall more appeare (as by this wast it will) that St. John's had it, but conceale the rest, they had it for their pennie. Wee beganne a suite with him the last tearme for the wast, but upon servinge of the writt, his stommack came downe, & now hee puts himself uppon the Colledges mercie, what to doe with him wee have not yet considered . . .[2]

. . . So expecting your Lordshipp's resolution for the building, with my praiers for the continuance of your health, I take my leave, ever resting

St. John's Oxon.   Your Lordshipp's to command
12° Martij 1631   Will^{ms} Juxon

---

[1] This library, which stood over a colonnade, had only recently been built, but proved to be structurally unsound and had to be demolished a few years later (*Victoria County History of* *Oxfordshire*, iii, 272).

[2] Thomas White, a member of the Founder's family, was the tenant of the College's estate at Fyfield in Berkshire.

To the right Honor[ble] and Reverend Father in God, my verie good Lord, the Lord Bysshopp of London, Chancelor of the Universitie of Oxford, at London house these bee deliverd.

[*Endorsed by Laud:*] Mar. 12 1631. The Chardge fullye cast of mye buildinge at St. John's in Oxford is to come to 3200[li].

My verie good Lord:

In the 3200[l] mentioned in my last letters, all charges whatsoever are included incident to the woorke both for materialls & woorkmanshipp in what kind soever, togeather with all alterations in the ould range & in this new: so that for the summe aforesaid, your Lordshipp shall have a perfect new Quadrangle made in all pointes which have beene hitherto in projection; the Librarie & the new range peiced out as manie feete as the Cloister can beare, & all passages fitted; so that the whole charge all manner of waies, shall not exceed 3200[l] in money & the 200 tunn of timber given.

We shall likewise in the woorke not charge your Lordshipp with more then 1700[l] for this yeare & also what was done the last; of which wee have receaved allredie 700[l], & I thinke I shall receave this afternoone 300[l] more of my Lord Bishopp of Oxford; & his Lordshipp upon the repaiment will deliver upp the acquittance which I make heere for the receipt, unto your Lordshipp . . .

So making bold upon the close of your Lordshipp's letters to proceede with the woorke after the forme last proiected with my praiers for your Lordshipp's health, I take my leave, ever resting

St. John's Oxon   Your Lordshipp's to command
19° Martij 1631   Will[mus] Juxon

To the right Honor[ble] and Reverend Father in god, my verie good Lord, the Lord Bishopp of London, Chancelor of the Universitie of Oxford, at London house these be delivered.

[*Endorsed by Laud:*] Mar. 19, 1631. Dr. Juxon's leter what my buildinge must cost me at S. Johns, exactlye cast up.

APPENDIX V

Articles of Agreement had made concluded and fuly agreed uppon the Second daie of May Anno domini 1633. In the Ninth yere of the raigne of our soveraigne Lord Charles by the grace of god king of England Scotland France and Ireland defender of the faith etc. Betweene the Right hon^ble and right reverend father in God William Lord Bishopp of London of the one parte And Hubert Le Sueur of London Sculpteur of the other parte whereby it is absolutelie covenanted concluded and agreed by and betweene the said parties to theis presents in manner and forme following (vizt).

In primis the said Hubert Le Sueur for him his executors and administrators doth covenante promise and graunte to and with the said William Lord Bishopp of London his executors and administrators by theis presents, That he the said Hubert Le Sueur or his assignes shall and will before the feast day of St. Michaell th' archangell which shalbe in the yeare of our Lord god one Thousand six hundred thirtie and fower substantially and workmanlike make and cast, or cause to be made and cast in brasse the Statue of our said soveraigne Lord King Charles six foote high. And the Statue of the Queenes Matie that nowe is in brasse likewise as bigg as the life.

In consideration whereof . . . the said Lord Bishopp of London . . . shall and will truly paie . . . to the said Hubert le Sueur . . . the somme of fower hundred pounds . . . in manner and forme following. That is to saie . . . One hundred pounds . . . before the insealing and delivery of theis presents, The receipt whereof the said Hubert le Sueur doth hereby acknowledge, the like sume of one hundred pounds more when the said worke shalbe ready to cast, And the somme of Twoe hundred pounds more . . . when both the said Statues shalbe finished without any farther deley, And that he the . . . Bishop of London . . . at his owne proper costs and charges shall and will fetch and cary away the said twoe Statues from the said Hubert le Sueur when they shalbe finished, and place them where he . . . will have them sett up without any charge to the said Hubert le Sueur but only with the assistance of his advice counsell and direction, and hand and helpe ioyned thereunto.

In witness whereof the said parties to theis Articles of Agreement have interchangeably sett their hands and seales the daie and yeres first above written.

Sealed and delivered in the presence of

Agidius Chaissius	John Coult
Simon Rolleston	Geo. Snaith
W^m. Bell	Guil: London[1]

---

[1] Le Sueur's signature has been torn off. In the receipt of 3 May 1634 he signs himself 'Huber le Sueur'.

Note: for Le Sueur's receipt for the second payment of £100, dated 3 May 1634, see PRO, SPD Charles I, vol. 267, fo. 27. A note by Laud dated 13 Dec. 1634 states that the agreement has been cancelled and the £400 paid.

75. Detail of the porch of St Mary's Church, Oxford, built in 1637

76. One of the bases of the porch of St Mary's Church, with rams' heads similar to those in the Canterbury Quadrangle

APPENDIX VI

THE PORCH OF ST MARY'S CHURCH, OXFORD

ST Mary's porch is closely linked with the Canterbury Quadrangle in date, style, and patronage. It was built in 1637 at the expense of Dr Morgan Owen (d. 1645), a well-beneficed Welsh clergyman who had been Laud's chaplain and was later to be Bishop of Llandaff. He was a member of Jesus College, and had been given a DD at the time of the royal visit to Oxford in August 1636.[1] The gift of the porch to the University church was presumably an acknowledgement of this honour.

The porch forms the main entrance to the church from the High Street. A pedimented niche containing a statue of the Virgin and Child rises dramatically through a larger segmental pediment supported by twisted Composite columns. These columns stand on bases ornamented with rams' heads similar to those in the Canterbury Quadrangle (Fig. 76). The statue itself stands on a semi-Gothic pedestal which breaks through the crown of the classical outer arch and assumes the character of a pendant. Within, a complex Gothic fan-vault rises from canted walls to cover the space between the arch and the fifteenth-century south door-way of the church[2] (Fig. 75).

This porch was built by John Jackson, the master mason who completed the Canterbury Quadrangle. The Vice-Chancellor's accounts show that he under-took to build it for £250 and was paid an extra £22, which 'was judged fit to bee given unto him beyond his bargaine'.[3] At his trial in 1644 Laud was accused of responsibility for the 'very scandalous statue of the Virgin Mary with Christ in her arms, set up in front of the new Church Porch of St. Mary's', and according to his own account he cited in his defence 'Mr. Bromfeeld who did that work'.[4] This was presumably Edward Bromfield, one of the master carpenters employed on the Canterbury Quadrangle,[5] but any responsibility that he may have had for the porch is unlikely to have extended beyond the carpentry of the roof and the provision of scaffolding. Indeed, it may be that Laud had confused him with his fellow-craftman Jackson, or perhaps with the joiner Woodfield, who also did stone-carving.[6] The matter is further complicated by the inclusion of the porch in the list of works attributed to the sculptor Nicholas Stone by his nephew Charles Stoakes. Stoakes says that it was 'desind and built' by his uncle.[7] How-ever, the Vice-Chancellor's accounts make it clear that it was in fact built by Jackson, and the probability is that the design either originated from the same source as the Canterbury Quadrangle or was provided by Jackson himself.

[1] For his career see *DNB*.

[2] For plans and illustrations see T. G. Jackson, *The Church of St Mary the Virgin, Oxford* (1897) and Royal Commission on Historical Monuments, *City of Oxford* (1939).

[3] A. Wood, *Life and Times*, iv, ed. A. Clark, Oxford Historical Society (1895), p. 56.

[4] *State Trials*, ed. T. B. Howell, iv (1816), pp. 474–5.

[5] He was responsible for all the carpenter's work of the east and west ranges (Building Accounts, p. 36).

[6] See above, p. 9.

[7] *The Note-book and Account-book of Nicholas Stone*, ed. W. L. Spiers, Walpole Society (1918–19), 137.

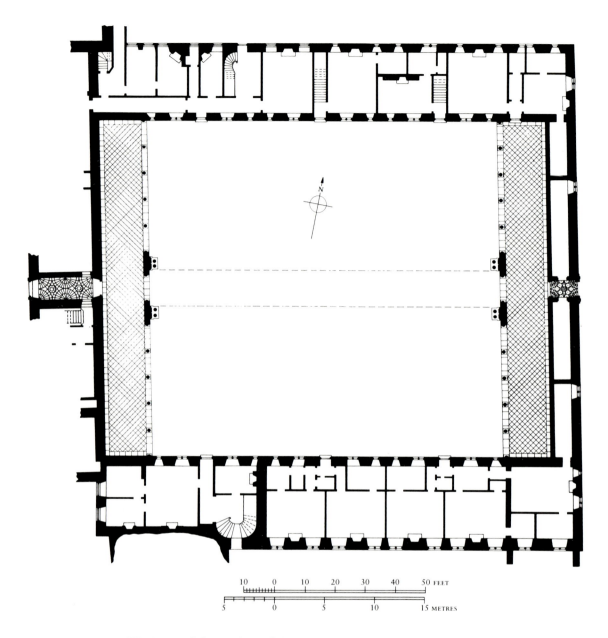

10   0   10   20   30   40   50 FEET

5   0   5   10   15 METRES

77. Ground-floor plan of the Canterbury Quadrangle *c*.1900

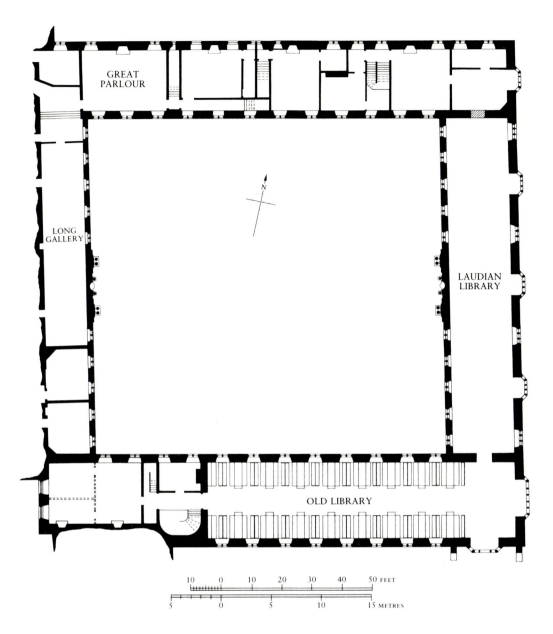

GREAT
PARLOUR

LONG
GALLERY

LAUDIAN
LIBRARY

OLD LIBRARY

N

10   0   10   20   30   40   50 FEET

5   0   5   10   15 METRES

78. First-floor plan of the Canterbury Quadrangle *c.*1900

INDEX